The Prophetic Voice in Modern Fiction

THE

PROPHETIC VOICE

IN MODERN FICTION

A HADDAM HOUSE BOOK BY

WILLIAM R. MUELLER

ASSOCIATION PRESS · NEW YORK

THE PROPHETIC VOICE IN MODERN FICTION

Library of Congress catalog card number: 59-6828

⬥ 475

Printed in the United States of America

For
Frances, Martha,
Mary, and Billy,
who suffered this book
to be written during
a summer "vacation"

PREFACE

To EDWARD L. NESTINGEN, editor of the *Intercollegian*, I am indebted for the general structure and procedure of this book. Mr. Nestingen submitted the manuscript idea for a study of this kind to the Haddam House Editorial Advisory Committee, which in turn asked me if I would develop the idea. I hope I have remained close enough to Mr. Nestingen's original suggestion so that he will not wish to disavow his brain child. At various stages along the way in my writing I have had helpful conversations with Warren H. Ashby and Marc Friedlaender, colleagues of mine at the Woman's College of the University of North Carolina; with William A. Lane of the Duke Divinity School; with J. Hillis Miller, Jr. of the Johns Hopkins University; and with my wife of the home. And it would be surprising if the happy influence of Nathan A. Scott, Jr., whose studies in literature and religion I have read carefully, is not noticed in the following pages.

To the students of my two freshman English classes at the Woman's College in the spring of 1958, I am grateful for their painstaking gathering of bibliographies of critical writings on various modern novelists, including those who are the subjects of this book; my students, despite their thoughtful and frequently voiced complaints, went about their assigned chore with faith, hope, and love. To Mrs. Marjorie Memory of the Woman's College Library for her industry in effecting some needed interlibrary loans, and to my former student Mrs. Diana Reed Jackson for her suggestion of the Dogberrian epigraph to the Graham Greene chapter, I wish to express my indebtedness. Perhaps most deserving of gratitude is Julian N. Hartt, who accepted the burden of reading and commenting upon the whole manuscript, a task which he carried out with tenacity; even in its final form the book is not, I suspect, all that Dr. Hartt would have wished, but it is considerably better than it would have been without his criticisms.

Finally I should like to acknowledge the publishing houses which have graciously consented to the use of quotations from novels published by them: The Viking Press for the Compass Book Edition of James Joyce's *A Portrait of the Artist as a Young Man*, and for Graham Greene's *The Heart of the Matter;* Alfred A. Knopf for Albert Camus' *The Fall*, translated by Justin O'Brien, and for the Definitive Edition of Franz Kafka's *The Trial*, translated by Willa and Edwin Muir; Random House for the Modern Library Edition of William Faulkner's *The Sound and the Fury;* and Harper & Brothers for Ignazio Silone's *A Handful of Blackberries*, translated by Darina Silone.

All biblical excerpts, unless otherwise indicated, are quoted from the *Revised Standard Version of the Bible*, copyrighted 1946 and 1952 by the Division of Christian Education, National Council of Churches, and used by permission.

WILLIAM R. MUELLER
The Woman's College of
The University of North Carolina

CONTENTS

The Prophetic Voice in Modern Fiction

INTRODUCTION

"I Have Used Similitudes"

Our wisdom, in so far as it ought to be deemed true and solid wisdom, consists almost entirely of two parts: the knowledge of God and of ourselves. But as these are connected together by many ties, it is not easy to determine which of the two precedes, and gives birth to the other. (Opening sentences of John Calvin's *Institutes of the Christian Religion*)

THIS BOOK WOULD NEVER HAVE BEEN WRITTEN without the conviction that a study of its subject matter, six modern novels and their relationship to the Bible, is worth the attention of any midtwentieth-century person who would grow in "true and solid wisdom." Wisdom remains, four hundred years after Calvin's definition, that knowledge of ourselves which convinces us of our sin and that knowledge of God which is our salvation. And it is frequently true that a man may come most directly to a knowledge of himself when he sees himself anatomized in a contemporary setting and in an idiom, a language, which is of his own time. The voices of the past few decades which have pierced most decisively to the heart of the matter, penetrating most deeply into the anxieties of our generation and expressing most precisely our fears and hopes, have been those of the literary artists, and it is perhaps above all in the modern

13

novel that we find the anatomy of our own age drawn with greatest clarity. The best of the twentieth-century novelists may with propriety lay claim to the title of latter-day prophets; for the health, or lack thereof, of our civilization is most accurately bodied forth in their words, just as the pulse of ancient Israel was most sensitively examined and expressed by the Old Testament prophets. Those of us who somehow suspect that all is not well, and who know that we are ill without knowing the temper of our disease, will find our condition nowhere more expertly diagnosed than in the pages of the most perceptive novelists of our time.

We should not infer from so strong a claim that the modern man in search of himself and of God can now lay aside his Bible and confidently turn for the revelatory and redeeming Word to the words of James Joyce or Albert Camus or Graham Greene or anyone else. To the Jew or Christian, the accuracy of any man's vision is always to be measured by that rule of truth which is the Bible. No one of the writers under discussion in this study is to be reckoned as a sturdy competitor of the Bible, but each has entered a fruitful dialogue with it. Indeed, most great works of art do complement the Bible, speaking directly to those who would be brought to a conviction of their sin and attesting to the fact that if God has at times been driven from this earth, he has not been driven out of existence. The serious student of modern fiction may discover that his reading eventuates in a self-knowledge alerting him to biblical affirmations which had previously gone unnoticed.

Rewarding dialogue between the Bible and the secular

work depends not upon the extent of their agreement regarding the nature of God and of man, but upon the degree of high seriousness, passionate intensity, and literary skill with which the secular work is presented. Works as different as Milton's *Paradise Regained* and Sartre's *No Exit*, for example, have in common with each other and with the Bible a deep concern for some ultimate answer to the mystery of existence. They propose radically different views of the meaning of life, but neither Milton nor Sartre could be said to grapple more seriously than the other with the most significant problems of man's existence and destiny. Milton finds an exit from our misery through the obedience and suffering of Jesus Christ; Sartre questions whether any Paradise has been lost, much less regained. Milton affirms the values which derive from the biblical tradition; Sartre finds no such values. Yet Sartre's nay and Milton's yea are addressed to the same constant, the western religious tradition whose source is the Bible; they are discoursing with the same protagonist. So pervasive is the biblical tradition in our culture that its affirmations are as eminently in our minds when we read Sartre as when we read Milton.

This present book is a study of certain thematic relationships between the Bible and six novels which proceed with high seriousness, passionate intensity, and literary skill in their search for the answers to our dilemmas. I have written primarily for those who have not yet come to grips with men who speak most directly to our unrest; for those who are seriously troubled by their seeming distance from the God whom they acknowledge as their Creator and seek as their Redeemer; for those who seek some knowledge, until now hidden from view, of the human condition and its spiritual potentialities. The story of our age is told most precisely and most eloquently in its imaginative literature, and if much of that literature points to the absence of man's encounter with God, it also points to the human situation which makes such an encounter so rare. The novels under study are hardly overflowing with a cheery optimism, but they serve as a sane counterbalance today to those desperate voices which invoke enthusiastically the "man up there," or argue that the frequent oral repetition of biblical phrases may persuade the Almighty to increase the incanter's sales-power, or suggest that a good deed a day keeps the devil away. Few of us would choose to live in Kafka's world or in Faulkner's, but if we in fact do live in a world of frustration and violence far removed from the Garden of Eden or the covers of the *Saturday Evening Post*, it is well that we know it. One can hardly reach a cherished destination if he does not know his point of departure. Our point of departure, I suspect, is most accurately chronicled by our novelists; our destination is the divine-human encounter which is our salvation. The novelist will not save us, but he may well bring us to the knowledge that we are in need of salvation.

In western civilization the great source book of man's meeting with God is the Bible, composed of sixty-six books written over a span of many centuries by many hands. Though the precise relationship between God and the various human spirits who penned the words of the biblical books is a matter of dispute, there is general agreement among Jews and Christians that their Bible (for the Jews this would be the Old Testament alone) was inspired by God in a way that cannot be claimed for any other work of literature. This means that for people of biblical faith the Bible is the definitive, though not necessarily the terminal, word about the relationship between God and man. But whatever one's theory (or lack of it) about biblical inspiration, and however largely one accepts or rejects the truth of the biblical proclamation, it is impossible for any writer to disengage himself from the profound influence which the Bible has had throughout many centuries: he may try to shout the Bible down, but he can hardly ignore it. If, as Whitehead suggested, the history of philosophy is a series of footnotes to Plato, then the history of religious thought in the West is a series of footnotes to the Bible, and it is difficult to find a literary work of consequence which does not bear the imprint of both. A great writer does not work in a cultural vacuum. Even if it were conceivable that he had never read the Bible, he would have fallen under its light or shadow if he had ever read anything or conversed with anybody.

If we accept Calvin's definition of wisdom as comprising a knowledge of God and of ourselves, we can seek that wisdom in Scripture and in those perceptive souls who, understanding most clearly the nature of God and of themselves, have been gifted with the power of communicating their experiences in writing. There are certain rugged individualists who would bypass both the Bible and the great literary expressions of man's struggle to know God and himself. These are the people who seek their religious nurture and self-understanding in the "One-impulse-from-a-vernal-wood" Academy, and who affirm that God reveals himself most accommodatingly in a sunset (or sunrise for those of more Spartan habits), a flower, a seashell, or a bird. Indeed, it is possible to grasp evidences of the Creator in his creation and to be brought to a sense of peace through an exposure to the natural world; and it is true that man can learn something of his own nature through observing natural processes. But the human being simply lacks those intuitive and imaginative graces which would enable him to come, through the perception of nature alone, to an understanding of his real condition and of his real relationship to God's laws and judgments and redemptive powers.

Furthermore, the human eye and ear and nose which find solace in the beauty of nature have almost invariably been conditioned by what they already know about the Creator and his creation through his Word, spelled out in the biblical books and in the person and works of Jesus Christ. If the finding of God or the knowledge of self can really be consummated through the rapturous embrace of nature alone, one of two things would seem to be true: either the Bible is not what the Judeo-Christian tradition claims it to be, or the Creator and Redeemer is a poor economist, wasting his time on such supererogatory activities as the inspiring of the Bible and the breaking into history (and out of it again) in the person of Jesus Christ.

Without undue deprecation of the place of nature in the religious experience and without denying that some persons may come to a mystical vision of God far from the public or university library, I am saying that the starting place in man's search for God or for himself is to be found for us in the written word. Our religious schooling is primarily literary, and we build upon the memories of those who have preceded us, memories of how God revealed himself and the human condition to man in history and through history. This book will be a study of some of those memories drawn from ancient and modern times.

Paul tells us that for the time being at least, we can see God only through a "dark glass." The Christian feels that the glass became less obscure with the Incarnation and that his vision of God may be a more complete one than, say, that of the Israelites who followed Moses out of Egypt. Until man sees God face to face, however, he must describe the religious experience in a language different from that of the natural scientist or the historian of the Civil War. And when he wishes to write his spiritual history and to tell of the invisible workings of the Holy Spirit which beckons to him and of the demons which beset him, he has to communicate these inner realities by translating them into outer actions and fashioning them forth in bold, dramatic, adventurous narratives. The demons may become dragons and monsters, and the good angels may become gallant knights and ladies fair; the lively outer action will reflect the inner frustrations and joys, the spiritual retrogression and progress of the protagonists.

Anyone acquainted with Book One of Edmund Spenser's *The Faerie Queene* will recall how the conquest of faith by the Red Cross Knight is reflected through his stirring physical adventures. And when John Bunyan wrote his story about a pilgrim named Christian who took a harrowing journey from a place called the City of Destruction to a place called the Celestial City, he borrowed from the prophet Hosea (12:10, KJV) a sentence which aptly describes both Spenser's literary method and his own: "I have used similitudes." Bunyan means by this that he has not written a scientific, factual, literal log of an historically real voyage, but that he has by means of an allegory (an extensive and elaborate simile or metaphor, a pointing to inner reality by means of outward action) come as close as his language can to telling how a man becomes convinced of his sinfulness, repents, and is redeemed. Pilgrim's journey from the sinful condition which dwells in the City of Destruction to the redeemed condition which abides in the Celestial City is the journey of the soul's purification, and the difficulty of the spiritual voyage is made clear by such physical obstacles as the Slough of Despond, Vanity Fair, the wicked monster Apollyon, and the Giant Despair with his Doubting Castle.

The persistence of the allegorical journey in literature is seen also in that greatest of literary works with a strictly Christian theme, Dante's *Divine Comedy*, which also makes use of similitudes, tracing as it does the spiritual progress of its narrator from the physical agonies of the Inferno through the cleansing activity of Purgatory and on to the Beatific Vision; his "journey," of course, was not real in the same sense as Boswell's peripatetic trip through the Northern Isles, but his journey is a magnificent similitude of what goes on in the souls of men. Most great works of literature, Christian and non-Christian, do relate the spiritual, and sometimes geographical, odyssey of a man in search of what is to him of ultimate value. Homer's Odysseus is well-named, and the *Odyssey* is a worthy prototype of the journeys of many men to different lands and different faiths.

The Bible is compounded of odysseys of men who, like Job, are in search of a just Redeemer. The search is narrated in terms of certain great themes, extending from that of creation to that of final judgment. Put in its simplest terms, the biblical epic is the story of God's creation of a good universe whose most abundantly endowed creature commits the sin of disobedience; God's justice demands punishment, yet his mercy provides redemption for those who repent; the repentant suffer, are graced with the power of love, and are ultimately raised up to God's eternal presence. The Bible tells this story of man's enduring relationship with God in explicit, concrete, and dramatic terms. We may come to an understanding of this relationship through an understanding of such central themes as creation, sin and redemption, justice and mercy, suffering and love, themes which appear and reappear in rich variation throughout our scriptural texts. However, if the Bible is the most perfect and definitive word about the divine-human encounter, it is not the only word. Men of vision have continued and will continue to write of the divine act of creation, of man's fall and depravity, of God's grace and man's redemption. They continue to express in various ways and through various similitudes the biblical proclamation, and they also continue to challenge it.

Every thoughtful person must go through a truly agonizing struggle to come to some understanding of ultimate reality and to some vision of God. Each one of us, I hope, will in his own way re-enact Jacob's wrestling with the angel at Peniel and will demand satisfaction before giving up the struggle. There is not the slightest doubt that the great works of literature are records of this struggle and may serve as directional markers of varying significance and assistance to us. The magnificent story of Job is the tale of Jacob expanded to epic proportions. The journey of an Odysseus or an Aeneas is not merely a geographical tour, but also a quest for understanding, as the classical convention of the descent into Hades clearly shows. The hell which Lear endures on the stormy heath is the struggle and the condition which makes a humble man of a proud one, a wise man of an ignorant one. The journey of Dante in the *Divine Comedy*, of Bunyan in *The Pilgrim's Progress*, of Kafka in *The Trial* and *The Castle*—all these show in their different ways the persistent wrestling of the human spirit to come to an understanding of its relationship to God.

This book narrates the ways whereby some of our most gifted twentieth-century novelists have turned their attention to a few of those basic problems which have haunted reflective persons since the beginning of mankind. They are the same problems which form the very roots of biblical thought; they are called, if one's vocabulary is primarily a biblical one, the problems of vocation, sin, judgment, suffering, love, and redemption. But whatever they may be called, they are, in fact, the themes of great contemporary writing just as they are the themes of the Old Testament and the New.

Two facts about twentieth-century expressions of religious thought are of particular relevance to this study. One is that relatively few contemporary writings of an explicitly religious nature would qualify as either great literature or profound religious thought. There is much pulp devoted to the mawkish expression of man's love for God, just as there is to man's love for woman. Much "religious" writing is sentimental; it titillates flabby and easily seduced emotions and offends the taste of anyone with either literary or religious sensibilities. The central religious situation, that of man confronted by God, has become so vulgarized by the combined efforts of television, cinema, jukebox, popular writer, and popular preacher that it is becoming increasingly difficult to discuss this situation in serious and mature terms. One reason a Dante or a Milton would be unlikely in this century is that the biblical situations and the biblical vocabulary have been so overworked and sentimentalized by superficial and inept artificers that the serious writer struggling with the same basic problems must resort to different situations and different vocabulary.

The other fact is that much of the best twentieth-century literature has as its most central concern the divine-human encounter—or the absence of it—even though the encounter is not expressed in explicit terms of man's meeting God. Thus when Kafka, for example, wishes to write about the problems of judgment and of man's anxiety in the face of judgment, he writes what may at first seem to be a purely secular story about a man summoned to court in his native city. In writing *The Trial*, Kafka might say with Bunyan, "I have used similitudes," though his similitudes are considerably less obvious than Bunyan's. In short, there is the paradoxical situation in which much of our ostensibly religious writing is hardly worth the time of a person seeking religious insights or aesthetic satisfaction, and in which the most profound religious writing is frequently to be found in works which may initially appear to have little or nothing to do with man's relationship to God. This paradox justifies an attempt at a book of this kind.

The six novels chosen for our study fulfill two qualifications: each one can stand on its intrinsic literary and aesthetic worth; each one is related to some significant biblical concept. But although each work has as its pervasive theme some aspect of man's encounter with, or alienation from, God, the author's manner of speaking, his use of similitudes, may at first appear strange to one unaccustomed to the various idioms of the best contemporary writing. In spite of, or perhaps because of, their similitudes, many of the most able writers of our century—and among them figures as diverse as James Joyce, Albert Camus, Franz Kafka, William Faulkner, Graham Greene, and Ignazio Silone—do in fact have as their central concerns the same questions and problems expressed by the writers of the Bible. We still have with us historians of the human spirit —prophets, if not evangelists and apostles—who, following earlier prophetic voices, analyze and chronicle the sickness of their own civilization and, at times, chart the narrow redemptive road. Men still write about the creation, about innocence and sin and damnation and redemption, about love and hate and indifference and compassion, about wrath and judgment and mercy. Other novels with other themes might have been selected for our study, though I think that the six which were selected will serve well to show

how the twentieth-century writer carries on the prophetic strain of past ages.

Each of the following chapters will move from a thematic discussion of the novel in question, to a study of the biblical proclamation on the same theme, to a consideration of the relationship between novel and Bible in regard to their understanding of the theme. In a sense we shall have a series of dialogues between biblical and modern writers. A dialogue calls for sympathetic ears as well as active tongues, and remains legitimate and fruitful only as long as each participant is more interested in understanding his relationship to the other than in hearing himself talk. Dialogue degenerates into monologue, perhaps two monologues, as soon as one participant becomes more concerned with what he wishes the other to be or to say than with what the other really is or is really saying. And before a critic can produce and direct any kind of dialogue between Bible and modern novel, he must listen to both with as much disinterestedness and attentiveness as he can muster.

I have gone about this study neither with the intention of enhancing immeasurably the reputation of the Bible by showing that even our modern sages have been influenced by its words, nor with the intention of seeing to it that certain modern novelists might at last receive the angelic halos or demonic horns hitherto unjustly denied them. I have tried only to let Bible and modern fiction speak freely from their own inner beings, and not to make an assault on the integrity of either. To do otherwise would be to fall to the most cardinal of literary sins, the dishonest manipulation of a literary work through forcing it to say what the critic might like to hear rather than allowing it to speak from the springs of its heart. Should a critic ever be tempted to do so, he might well recall John Milton's assertion that "a good book is the precious life-blood of a master-spirit, embalmed and treasured up on purpose to a life beyond life."

It would perhaps be immodest to suggest that a reading of these pages before us will set all hearts at rest, and that the keys to the kingdom will be found in a small, rust-proof envelope attached to the bottom of the last page. But I would urge again that one road to that "true and solid wisdom" of which Calvin speaks may be found through the pages of the novels which here fall under our scrutiny. From the testimony of those writers who have seen most clearly the human situation and have disclosed the anatomy of modern man through their similitudes we may learn much. And self-knowledge figures prominently in the consummation of our ultimate goal, the divine-human encounter which is our salvation.

1.

THE THEME OF VOCATION:

James Joyce's *A Portrait of the Artist as a Young Man*

Don't give in too quickly to those who want to alleviate your anxiety about truth. Don't be seduced into a truth which is not really your truth, even if the seducer is your church, or your party, or your parental tradition. Go with Pilate, if you cannot go with Jesus; but go in seriousness with him. (Paul Tillich, "What Is Truth?" *The New Being*, Charles Scribner's Sons, 1955, pp. 67-68.)

I

—What is your name?
Stephen had answered: Stephen Dedalus.
Then Nasty Roche had said:
—What kind of a name is that?
And when Stephen had not been able to answer . . . (8-9)*

James Joyce might have subtitled his novel "A Young Man in Search of His Name," for *A Portrait of the Artist as a Young Man* is in great part the story of a perceptive human being who is trying to find out who he is and what

---

*In this chapter, all excerpts from *A Portrait of the Artist as a Young Man* by James Joyce are used by the permission of the publisher, The Viking Press, Inc., New York. Page references are to the Compass Book Edition, 1956.

he is supposed to be; Stephan Dedalus is in search of his calling, his vocation. Had Nasty Roche asked his questions at the end of the novel instead of at its beginning, Stephen could have obliged him with a detailed answer to "What kind of a name is that?" Stephen's eloquent description of his schoolmate at Clongowes Wood is evidence that he knew Nasty Roche before he knew himself: "Nasty Roche was a stink." (8)

Stephen's acute sensitivity to language in general—note, for example, his disquisitions upon the words "belt" and "suck" in the early pages of the novel—is particularly evident in regard to proper nouns, to names of persons and of places. He recalls that Dante Riordan "had taught him where the Mozambique Channel was and what was the longest river in America and what was the name of the highest mountain in the moon" (11). And in his early school days, struggling vainly to learn American place names, he had turned for solace to his own notations on his geography book:

> *Stephen Dedalus*
> *Class of Elements*
> *Clongowes Wood College*
> *Sallins*
> *County Kildare*
> *Ireland*
> *The World*
> *The Universe* (16)

It concerned him a little that he could not go beyond the universe; he knew, of course, that nothing came after the universe, but he was not certain where the universe ended and where nothing began. Only the mind of God could solve such problems, a thought which led him to the conclusion that "God was God's name just as his name was Stephen"—even though the French called God *Dieu* (16). When, some years later, Stephen accompanied his father to Cork, he was again preoccupied with names and found that the memory of his childhood was reduced to names:

> —I am Stephen Dedalus. I am walking beside my father whose name is Simon Dedalus. We are in Cork, in Ireland. Cork is a city. Our room is in the Victoria Hotel. Victoria and Stephen and Simon. Simon and Stephen and Victoria. Names.
>
> The memory of his childhood suddenly grew dim. He tried to call forth some of its vivid moments but could not. He recalled only names. Dante, Parnell, Clane, Clongowes. (92)

One of the most memorable episodes from Stephen's first and exceedingly memorable Christmas dinner was Mr. Casey's "story about a very famous spit." Mr. Casey, once making his way to the railway station at Arklow after having attended a meeting presided over by his chief and idol Parnell, was accosted by a drunken old woman who assailed him with all kinds of names.

> —Well. I let her bawl away, to her heart's content, *Kitty O'Shea* and the rest of it till at last she called that lady a name that I won't sully this Christmas board nor your ears, ma'am, nor my own lips by repeating. (37)

He had obliged the old woman by a mouthful of tobacco juice in the eye. Stephen's curiosity about the name which Mr. Casey would not repeat was never satisfied.

Also related to the concept of names was the most humiliating experience of Stephen's early schooling. Not only had Father Dolan unjustly stung his palm with the pandybat; he had twice asked him his name, an unforgivable insult.

> He thought of the baldy head of the prefect of studies with the cruel nocoloured eyes looking at him and he heard the voice of the prefect of studies asking him twice what his name was. Why could he not remember the name when he was told the first time? Was he not listening the first time or was it to make fun out of the name? The great men in the history had names like that and nobody made fun of them. It was his own name that he should have made fun of if he wanted to make fun. Dolan: it was like the name of a woman who washed clothes. (55-56)

Stephen did not share his father's insensitivity to names and would never, like him, have said, " 'Tim or Tom or whatever your name is.' " (95)

The importance to Stephen of names, particularly of his own name, is tremendous, because a name is to him not simply a sound or an utterance to attract the attention of its bearer. A person *is* his name, and he has to discover the meaning of his name in order to discover the meaning of himself. For Stephen to tell Nasty Roche that he did not know what kind of name Stephen Dedalus was, was to tell Nasty that he did not know himself. Joyce's novel traces Stephen's growing awareness of who he is and what he should be. In other words, it is a novel of vocation: what Stephen was called is the key to Stephen's calling. This insistence on being true to his name and to himself guarded

him from being lured by a number of false calls: the call
of his family to remain within its bosom; the call of the
Church to be ordained into her priesthood; the call of his
zealous, chauvinistic schoolmates to carry the banner of
Irish nationalism.

Each of the novel's five chapters ends on an ecstatic note,
and each note is a resolution of some inner tension related
to Stephen's decision about the meaning of his name. In-
dignant at Father Dolan's brutality, injustice, and disrespect
to his name, Stephen at the end of Chapter One goes to
Father Conmee, Rector of Clongowes Wood, to inform on
Father Dolan, despite Simon Dedalus' instructions to his
son never to peach on anyone. Not only does the rector
know Stephen's name without being told; he also promises
to speak to Father Dolan. Stephen, his pride in his name
vindicated, returns to his fellows "happy and free" and with
a joy-giving sense of condescension toward the wielder
of the pandybat.

Chapter Two traces Stephen's growing estrangement
from his family. The bearers of his own name are of no
positive help in his search for his destiny. As his family
proudly awaits him at the conclusion of his dramatic per-
formance at school, he runs by them, fabricating an excuse
to flee from them. And his trip with Mr. Dedalus to Cork
serves only to substantiate his view of his father as a
coarse, insensitive person who embarrasses him with his
adolescent sense of humor and his extroverted flirtatiousness
and talkativeness. His father's sense of vocation—that one
should be above all a good fellow, should be a good singer,
a good actor, a good oarsman, a good racket player, or a

good storyteller—was completely alien to his own deeper sense of calling. Try as he might to be a sympathetic member of his own family, to feel a call to a united family life, Stephen had to confess his failure:

> He saw clearly . . . his own futile isolation. He had not gone one step nearer the lives he had sought to approach nor bridged the restless shame and rancour that had divided him from mother and brother and sister. He felt that he was hardly of the one blood with them but stood to them rather in the mystical kinship of fosterage, foster child and foster brother. (98)

If he had been driven from Father Dolan to Father Conmee, he was now driven from his family to a prostitute. Improperly recognized by his family, unable to surrender his being and his love to them, he found his solace and ecstasy in a whore's embrace:

> He closed his eyes, surrendering himself to her, body and mind, conscious of nothing in the world but the dark pressure of her softly parting lips. They pressed upon his brain as upon his lips as though they were the vehicle of a vague speech; and between them he felt an unknown and timid pressure, darker than the swoon of sin, softer than sound or odour. (101)

Chapter Three narrates another call made upon Stephen and shows his turning from the words of the prostitute ("Give me a kiss") to the words of the priest ("*Corpus Domini nostri*"), from the arms of the harlot to those of his Lord, from "soft perfumed flesh" to the very Body of God in the celebration of the Eucharist. The change was effected by means of a retreat in honor of St. Francis Xavier, patron of Stephen's college. The sermons which so stirred Stephen's soul were eschatological, were on the topics of death, judgment, hell, and heaven. He learned that man's one end is to do God's will and to save his soul, and that Lucifer was cast from heaven because of his sinful thought, "*Non serviam:* I will not serve." The sermons, relating in terrible fashion the tribulation that will be visited upon those who will not serve, brought to Stephen a full conviction of the sins of his flesh and led him to the confessional. Contrite in heart, he confessed, was absolved by the priest and, on the following day, free from the weight of his mortal sins he found a new peace, a new ecstasy, this time in the Eucharist. In a greater exaltation than either Father Conmee or the prostitute could give him, Stephen was convinced that the call of God, as spoken through the Mass, would hold him eternally: "Another life! A life of grace and virtue and happiness! It was true. It was not a dream from which he would awake. The past was past." (146)

God's call to Stephen through the Mass does not hold him eternally, but this "conversion" is a necessary step in Stephen's search for himself. Participation in the Eucharist and the asceticism which immediately followed were the antithesis to his former life, leading ultimately to the synthesis which is yet to come. If the life which immediately preceded the retreat was one of license and dissipation of the senses, that which immediately followed was one of most rigid and painstaking mortification. We learn early in Chapter Four that Stephen walked with downcast eyes, avoiding especially the eyes of women; that he subjected his ears to the most cacophonous and strident sounds; that he deliberately sought out the most revolting smells; that he observed strictly the fasts of the church; and that he welcomed the greatest discomfort to his sense of touch. Even so, he found himself still at the mercy of the passions of anger and loathing.

To the outward eye, however, Stephen had amended his life, so much so that the director of his college urged him to heed the vocation of the priesthood. Characteristically, Stephen had a vision of his name, "The Reverend Stephen Dedalus, S.J.," but this vision, which would have moved him to joy after the retreat, was now followed by the image of a face that was "eyeless and sourfavoured and devout, shot with pink tinges of suffocated anger" (161). He envisioned the life of the priesthood as "grave and ordered and passionless" (160), and he was repelled by its "chill and order" (161), an order which, in his view, brought constraint rather than freedom, lifelessness rather than passionate intensity, and which minimized one's individuality. His long-standing conviction of his difference from all other persons led him to seek his destiny and wisdom elsewhere and alone: "He was destined to learn his own wisdom apart from others or to learn the wisdom of others himself wandering among the snares of the world." (162)

It is a fine irony that Stephen should be made aware of his destiny not by the call of the priest, but by the bantering calls of his schoolmates, boisterously playing as they swam in the river. Stephen's name was not the Reverend Stephen Dedalus, S.J., but the name formed by the lips of his friends: "—Stephanos Dedalos! Bous Stephanoumenos! Bous Stephaneforos." This, finally, was his call.

> . . . Now, as never before, his strange name seemed to him a prophecy. . . . Now, at the name of the fabulous artificer, he seemed to hear the noise of dim waves and to see a winged form flying above the waves and slowly climbing the air. What did it mean? Was it a quaint device opening a page of some medieval book of prophecies and symbols, a hawklike man flying sunward above the sea, a prophecy of the end he had been born to serve and had been following through the mists of childhood and boyhood, a symbol of the artist forging anew in his workshop out of the sluggish matter of the earth a new soaring impalpable imperishable being? (168-169)

Stephen's real descent was, indeed, not from Simon Dedalus, but from the Greek Daedalus, that "fabulous artificer" who had contrived the ingenious Labyrinth as a trap for the Minotaur in Crete. And Daedalus was more than an unrivaled architect; he was a clever and wise man who could escape from the very maze which confined all others. When King Minos had imprisoned him within the Labyrinth of his own making, Daedalus, unable to go through the maze, had outwitted Minos by flying freely into the air. Stephen was his true kin in two ways: he was to be an artist, "forging anew in his workshop out of the sluggish matter of the earth a new soaring impalpable imperishable being"; and he was to escape from his own labyrinth, the stultifying maze of family, church, and nation. Stephen was now flying sunward and, in retrospect, he saw his childhood and boyhood for the mists that they were; neither the joyful swoon in the embrace of the

prostitute nor even the Eucharistic entry of God into his
body had moved him to so complete a surrender. It was
Stephen's vision of Daedalus which called his soul to an
ecstasy of flight compared to which all his former calls
were "but the cerements shaken from the body of death";
the utterance of the name of the hawklike man—"This was
the call of life to his soul not the dull gross voice of the
world of duties and despair, not the inhuman voice that had
called him to the pale service of the altar." (169)

Stephen had by now gone far on the journey through
that alembic which was to make of him the artist which was
his calling, and the reader can see the first sign of the synthesis of his voyage as Stephen beheld a lovely girl in a
stream. Stephen viewed her with the eye of the artist; the
relationship between his whole self and the object beheld
was the relationship which makes artistic creation possible.
Stephen had viewed the prostitute purely as an object of
desire; his aim was the gratification of his senses. The antithesis to this disposition of the senses was found immediately
after the retreat when Stephen sought to eradicate all his
desires; his aim then was the mortification of his senses.
But now he sought neither gratification nor mortification.
He was stirred neither to possess the body nor to avoid the
eyes of the girl. His gaze was worshipful, and the girl
returned his gaze "without shame or wantonness" (171).
He experienced the reality of stasis, which underlies the
aesthetic he develops in the last chapter. The girl, who
would have stirred him to wantonness at one time, to withdrawal at another, and who in the eyes of the insensitive
might indeed be merely "the sluggish matter of the earth,"

became through the eyes of the new Stephen "a new soaring impalpable imperishable being."

Stephen could now answer Nasty Roche; he now knew what kind of name Stephen Dedalus was. His vision of the young girl was the first concrete manifestation that he had found his true self and that he was responding according to the nature, demands, and genius of this self. He turned from the girl "crying to greet the advent of the life that had cried to him" (171). Joyously he responded to the call which he knew to be his own:

> Her eyes had called him and his soul had leaped at the call. To live, to err, to fall, to triumph, to recreate life out of life! A wild angel had appeared to him, the angel of mortal youth and beauty, an envoy from the fair courts of life, to throw open before him in an instant of ecstasy the gates of all the ways of error and glory. On and on and on and on! (172)

Chapter Five is both a summation of the novel and a statement of the precise nature of Stephen's calling. Stephen is impressed again by the unloveliness of his family, his church, and his nation. His estrangement from his family is underlined in the early pages of the chapter. And the priesthood, which had almost laid claim on his life, is characterized by the dean of studies of his university who, despite his years of outward service to the Lord, remained in body at least "ungraced by aught of saintly or of prelatic beauty." Servant of God as he appeared to be, he had never felt a call to his innermost soul, and his "mortified will [was] no more responsive to the thrill of its obedience than was to the thrill of love or combat his aging body.

. . ." Lacking in spirit and vitality, he was loveless, passionless, joyless (185-186). As for his nation, Stephen viewed
the Irish as batlike souls (183, 238) fettered in darkness.
His relation to Ireland is Daedalus' relation to the Labyrinth—"When the soul of a man is born in this country
there are nets flung at it to hold it back from flight"—and
he will try to fly by the nets of "nationality, language,
religion" (203). Stephen realized that the call of the fabulous
artificer would take him from his home, his nation, his
communion, and it is possible that, when he recited his
own creed, he remembered the retreat sermon in which
Lucifer's sin was succinctly phrased: "*Non serviam:* I will
not serve." Stephen is no longer the person he was when he
rejoiced in the ecstasy of the post-retreat communion;
his new creed he recited to Cranly:

> I will not serve that in which I no longer believe,
> whether it call itself my home, my fatherland, or my
> church: and I will try to express myself in some mode of
> life or art as freely as I can and as wholly as I can, using
> for my defence the only arms I allow myself to use—
> silence, exile, and cunning. (247)

Stephen's mode of life will be that of the artist, and his
medium will be literature, "the highest and most spiritual
art" (214). The genius of the artist, the quality that makes
the man an artist, that enables the man to know that the
call of Daedalus is the call to him, is his vision, his way of
looking at the creation. He becomes so absorbed by the
object which he beholds that he is somehow forgetful of
self. His mind is possessed or, as Stephen says, "arrested"
by the object in such a way that he is moved neither to

desire nor to loathing (205). When Stephen's friend Lynch
derived pleasure from penciling his name on the buttocks
of the Venus of Praxiteles, he was not responding with the
soul of an artist. When Stephen saw the young girl in the
stream and was arrested by the loveliness of her being, he
was exercising the artist's vision.

The artist's imagination is a purifying vessel, bringing
"out of the sluggish matter of the earth a new soaring impalpable imperishable being." As such, he is a creator of a
kind, accomplishing a mystery like that of God's work in
early Genesis (215). More than this, the artist's imagination
is like the womb of the Virgin Mary, and as God caused
the Word to become flesh, so does the artist fashion forth
through words the product of his vision, the truth of creation—"In the virgin womb of the imagination the word
was made flesh" (217). And even beyond this, the artist
performs a miracle like that of the priest as he pronounces
the words of institution and consecration before the altar;
there is in art a sacramental function—the artist is "a priest
of eternal imagination, transmuting the daily bread of experience into the radiant body of everlasting life." (221)

The Stephen who leaves us at the end of the novel is not
yet the mature artist, but he is a person who has been
possessed by a call, who has discovered the meaning of his
name, and who is ready to set out like the young Milton
"to fresh woods, and pastures new." The hand of Daedalus
has been set upon him, and he stands ready to surrender
himself to the life of the artist. The last two entries in his
diary are a statement of intent and an invocation to his
saint: "Welcome, O life! I go to encounter for the millionth

time the reality of experience and to forge in the smithy of my soul the uncreated conscience of my race. . . . Old father, old artificer, stand me now and ever in good stead." (253)

II

Shakespeare's "A rose by any other name is just as sweet" shows that his olfactory sense was keener than his theological acumen. The latter is more in evidence when Juliet Capulet, a young lady given to various excesses, would not rest content with a single vocative: "O Romeo, Romeo! wherefore art thou Romeo?" She knew instinctively the loveliness of naming. The importance of naming and of calling by name are nowhere more emphatic than in the biblical tradition. We learn in the third chapter of Exodus that when Jahweh first wished to speak with Moses, he did not whistle at him and did not call out, "Hey you"; the Lord's first words to Moses were "Moses, Moses." And the startled, shy, and diffident Moses knew the futility of carrying God's message to the Israelites unless he could also tell them the name of the Being who commissioned him to lead the chosen ones out of their bondage in Egypt; one of his first questions was to ask God his name. Jahweh is not simply the God of Abraham, Isaac, and Jacob; he is also "I am who I am." Or, to view this brief dialogue in another and a paradoxical way, the *one* God is the *only* Being and consequently has no need of a personal name. He is Being Itself—"I am who I am."

In Old Testament thought the power to name is closely related to the power to create. The opening verses of

Genesis show God not only as creator but also as namer. After he decreed that there be light, he "called the light Day, and the darkness he called Night." One of his greatest evidences of favor to Adam and one of the real marks of Adam's original majesty was Jahweh's gracious appointment of the first man to name all the birds of the air and the beasts of the field: He "brought them to the man [Adam] to see what he would call them; and whatever the man called every living creature, that was its name" (Genesis 2:19). The ancient biblical writers believed that the bestowal of a name was necessary for the object named to gain its full measure of existence; in this sense, the bestower is a kind of creator, endowing the named with a fullness of life and granting it or him an individuality. The namer thus has a power over the named, and God has a power over his total creation as Adam has over all the non-human creatures of the earth. To say that Adam named the creatures is simply another way of saying that man was to "have dominion over the fish of the sea, and over the birds of the air, and over the cattle, and over all the earth, and over every creeping thing that creeps upon the earth." (Genesis 1:26)

A proper name in the Bible is also indicative of the character or personality of the person; far more than being a mere sound whose utterance summons or calls attention to its bearer, a name indicates his nature and destiny. Jahweh, having destined the first patriarch to have descendants as manifold as the particles of dust of the earth or as the stars of the heavens, changes his name from Abram to Abraham, from "exalted father" to "father of a multitude." Sarai becomes Sarah, meaning "princess," and the son of her old age is named Isaac, meaning "he laughs" and resulting from the fact that both Abraham and Sarah, knowing that her natural life was beyond childbirth, laughed when the angel of the Lord had announced the coming of her son.

There is perhaps no story in the Old Testament of greater relevance to the significance of names than that of Jacob's nocturnal wrestling match, related in the thirty-second chapter of Genesis. He was facing a real crisis as he prepared to meet his brother, Esau, strongly armed and with every good reason to seek his younger twin's destruction. It was the night before their meeting when Jacob was alone and wrestled until daybreak with a strange assailant. His opponent, unable to overpower him, asked Jacob to release him, and Jacob refused to do so until his opponent conferred his blessing. "What is your name?" asked the strange one, indicating that he had to know *whom* he was blessing. And when Jacob answered, the wrestler said, " 'Your name shall no more be called Jacob, but Israel [meaning "He who strives with God" or "God strives"], for you have striven with God and with men, and have prevailed.' " Jacob then asked the wrestler's name, and the latter blessed him but did not verbally reveal his name. But Jacob suddenly knew that his opponent, namer, and blesser was God himself, and he named the place of the combat Peniel, meaning "the face of God." This wonderfully exciting story is more than a good narrative. It is an indication that Jacob has with courage and tenacity weathered a crisis and is destined to carry on the blessed roles of Abraham and Isaac as leader of the Israelites. His nature and destiny is found in his name—Israel; he will not be overcome by Esau.

That naming is an important concept in the New Testament also is shown, for example, in the play upon Simon Peter's name. In the Fourth Gospel Jesus comments on Peter's name at their first meeting: " 'So you are Simon the son of John? You shall be called Cephas' (which means Peter)" (1:42). The significance of the statement lies in the fact that the Greek word *petra* means rock. At Caesarea Philippi Christ makes the most of this word play just after Peter has identified him as the Son of the living God: " 'And I tell you, you are Peter, and on this rock I will build my church, and the powers of death shall not prevail against it.' " (Matthew 16:18)

The biblical God not only names his creatures; he also calls them. He calls Adam to punishment, Noah to the building of the ark, and Abram to a new land away from his own country and his kindred. He calls the great prophets and makes known to them through visions what he expects of them in the life of their times. It will suffice to note God's call to and encounter with two of his chosen servants, Moses and Saul-Paul.

The story of Moses by the burning bush and his confrontation by the Lord is a familiar one. Tending his father-in-law's sheep on Mount Horeb, his amazed attention was riveted on a burning bush that was not consumed. As he looked with fascination upon this curious spectacle, the voice of the Lord called to him out of the bush, saying, " 'Do not come near; put off your shoes from your feet, for the place on which you are standing is holy ground' "

(Exodus 3:5). There follows a dialogue through which Jahweh makes clear to Moses precisely what service he is being called upon to effect. Moses is to act as God's instrument to lead the enslaved, chosen Israelites out of their Egyptian bondage and on toward the Promised Land. Moses is resourceful in conjuring up reasons for not accepting the call. Who is he to undertake this tremendous task? Who is he to say sent him when the Israelites ask on whose authority he assumes leadership? What, indeed, are his credentials, and how is he to persuade his people that "I am" really appeared to him? How is he, so ineloquent and slow of speech, to communicate this earthshaking message? Can't God find someone else to heed his call and do the job? Moses is as ingenious as most of us in trying to persuade himself that it would be better not to follow God's call— he is fully satisfied tending Jethro's sheep on Mount Horeb. But he finally unenthusiastically accepts Jahweh's commission and contends at great length with Pharaoh, who is as tenacious in his way as Job was in his. The plagues, the Passover, the crossing of the Red Sea, the sweetening of the water of Marah, the provision of quail and manna, the springing of water from the rocks at Horeb—all these mighty acts of the Lord serve as the credentials of Moses while his people, wavering in faith and in courage, urge a forsaking of this journey and a return to a bondage the known discomforts of which seem preferable to the unknown terrors which appear to lie ahead. After the Israelites had entered the wilderness of Sinai, the Lord summoned Moses again, this time to the top of the mountain for the revelation of God's Law. Despite the continued restiveness and faithlessness of the people, the fashioning of the idolatrous golden calf, and the breaking of the tablets engraved with the Ten Commandments, Moses stands fast as God's servant and is the instrument of freedom for his people. The story of Moses is that of the servant who grudgingly yet faithfully answers God's call. He is the forerunner of the prophetic tradition and affords us the most comprehensive example of the meaning of a called one in Old Testament literature.

The irony of Saul's conversion, which Luke sees fit to narrate three times (Chapters 9, 22 and 26 of the Acts of the Apostles), is that Saul felt completely possessed by a calling before his trip toward Damascus. He was, as he tells us in Philippians 3:5-6, "circumcised on the eighth day, of the people of Israel, of the tribe of Benjamin, a Hebrew born of Hebrews; as to the law a Pharisee, as to zeal a persecutor of the church, as to righteousness under the law blameless." He was the most faithful of members of the most law-abiding and God-fearing people who ever lived; he built no golden calves and broke no tablets, but rather was one who might have convinced Moses that his own service to Jahweh had borne rich fruit. It was in answer to what Saul felt to be God's call that he consented to Stephen's death and, later, "breathing threats and murder against the disciples of the Lord" (Acts 9:1), set out for Damascus to arrest those followers of a false Messiah who were desecrating the ways of God. But it was then he learned that what he took to be his call was a false one. A flash of light felled him on his journey, and a voice called him by name: " 'Saul, Saul, why do you persecute me?' "

When Saul asked the identity of the speaker, he was told, " 'I am Jesus, whom you are persecuting; but rise and enter the city, and you will be told what you are to do.' " Struck blind, he was taken to Damascus, where the disciple Ananias was told by the Lord to lay hands on Saul that his sight might be restored. When Ananias protested any succoring of the infamous enemy of Christ, the Lord related that Saul was his chosen instrument and that he would show Saul "how much he must suffer for the sake of my name." The constant in Saul's relationship to God is his conviction both before and after the conversion that he is serving God; the variable is his concept of the nature of this service. Saul, to be known as Paul in his service to the Father of the Lord Jesus Christ, becomes convinced that the Lord has for the first time revealed to him the true nature of his calling—suffering and service for the cross of Christ.

The contemporary meaning which we attribute to the word "calling" or "vocation"—namely the particular occupation or profession at which one labors and earns his livelihood—is more a heritage from Luther and the Reformation than from the biblical tradition. The "called" of the New Testament are specifically those who have been called to repentance and, usually, those who have been elected to salvation. Paul tells us in the first chapter of Romans that he was "called to be an apostle, set apart for the gospel of God," that is, called to salvation and to the preaching of the salvation message to others; he is writing to those persons in Rome "who are called to be saints," not called to be Christian butchers, bakers, and candlestick makers. The

New Testament concept of the called is most clearly expressed in Romans 8:28-30:

> We know that in everything God works for good with those who love him, who are called according to his purpose. For those whom he foreknew he also predestined to be conformed to the image of his Son, in order that he might be the first-born among many brethren. And those whom he predestined he also called; and those whom he called he also justified; and those whom he justified he also glorified.

Luther's zeal to undermine the power of the Papacy is in great part responsible for our own view of Christian vocation. Alarmed by the papal claim to a spiritual power which was above the temporal power of the German nation, he wrote in his *Open Letter to the Christian Nobility of the German Nation* that all Christians, priests, and laymen alike, are members of the "spiritual estate," that all Christians are consecrated to the priesthood, and that civil power should rest in the hands of civil authorities. Lay people are no less Christians, no less called, than priests; the differences among Christians are simply those of office. Citing I Corinthians 12, Luther points out that all Christians are of one body, each with his own work in service to all others. Again, in *The Babylonian Captivity of the Church,* Luther seeks to whittle down the priestly power, particularly the view that the priest enjoys a particular favor in the eyes of God and that his calling is more Christian than other callings. Luther affirms that the works of the priest find no more favor with God than those of the rustic in the fields or the woman in her household tasks. Devotion to God is measured not by the nature of one's calling, but by the presence of faith in whatever calling a man may find himself.

Calvin's view of vocation, which also was instrumental in shaping our view, is summed up in his *Institutes of the Christian Religion*, III, x, 6:

> . . . The Lord enjoins every one of us, in all the actions of life, to have respect to our own calling. . . . And that no one may presume to overstep his proper limits, he has distinguished the different modes of life by the name of callings . . . in following your proper calling, no work will be so mean and sordid as not to have a splendour and value in the eye of God.

Thus, with the thought of the Reformation, the word "called" gained a more comprehensive meaning. If the New Testament affirms a call to salvation, the Reform writers speak of a calling as that particular earthly work through which one may manifest the kind of faith and devotion which marks him as one of God's elect.

III

Yet to confront us is the problem, fascinating and complex, of the relationship between the concept of vocation suggested by the novel and that implied or stated in the biblical tradition. A subdivision of this problem is the distinguishing among Stephen's judgment on his vocational decision and its bearing on his salvation, Joyce's judgment, and the judgment of the reader standing outside the novel. The preacher at the retreat stated succinctly that a person's reason for being and his sole purpose and calling in this world were "to do God's holy will and to save [his] immortal soul" (109-110); he later defined Satan's first and fatal sin as his unwillingness to serve (117) and pronounced the terrible words of rejection which would fall upon Satan's followers: "*Depart from me, ye cursed, into everlasting fire which was prepared for the devil and his angels!*" (124). Did Stephen answer God's call to serve or Lucifer's call not to serve? Was the call of the mythological Daedalus the call of the Lord or of Satan?

The answer of the Roman Catholic Church (an answer with which Stephen and Joyce were of course quite familiar) is that the Stephen who goes into exile at the end of the novel is, for the time being at least, a lost soul. He is lost not because he rejects the priesthood; his call to the priesthood was a false one (for one thing, he had been attracted to it in part for the wrong reason—his desire for its awful power and authority), and there is no question about the possibility of the salvation of an artist. But the salvation must come within the framework of the Church —Protestant, if not Catholic—and Stephen has rejected not only the priesthood but the Church itself. Following the Sacrament of Penance in which Stephen confessed his sin of the flesh, "his prayers ascended to heaven from his purified heart like perfume streaming upwards from a heart of white rose" (145); at that time, even though the purple prose might suggest some sentimentality in Stephen's response, nevertheless the disposition of his heart would affirm a positive relationship to God through the sacramental rite. But when Stephen later confessed to Cranly his agnostic attitude toward the Eucharist (239) and his lack of faith in the Church (247), he was severing himself from God's grace. He was refusing the sacrament to which all Christians are called and was consequently turning a deaf ear to his Christian calling. From the point of view of the Church, Stephen by the end of the novel is at best a prodigal son who may or may not return. Like Lucifer, Stephen is one who will not serve—or, at least, will not serve through the instrument which God has ordained for His service, the Church or the Body of Christ.

From the Reformed Protestant view as well, Stephen is one who remains outside the communion of saints, for he is not one of the priesthood of believers. However much he may devote himself to the calling of the artist, he is following his vocation apart from the Christian community as it manifests itself in the Body of Christ. If Luther and Calvin saw a more comprehensive meaning in the word "calling" than that which is explicit in the New Testament, they nevertheless insisted that the varieties of gifts which come from God are to be accompanied by God's call to his Church and to be used within the framework of the One Body.

This is to say that the orthodox Christian reader, Catholic or Protestant, would, by juxtaposing the pronouncements of his religious tradition on the matter of vocation and Stephen's words and actions, see Stephen as outside the realm of grace. Yet there is a real question whether the reader finishes his reading of the novel with the judgment to which orthodoxy would seem to lead. The novel's use of both pagan and biblical reference and imagery sometimes leads us in quite another direction. For example, when Stephen comes upon his companions swimming, hears them call his name, and envisions the great Daedalus, his ecstasy is translated in both biblical and pagan terms. The vision delivers him from the bondage of his past, including his bondage to the Church. In Stephen's view his old self, with all its fear, incertitude, and shame, dies within him and frees his soul for its true calling. He shakes off the "cerements, the linens of the grave"; he is convinced that his soul has "arisen from the grave of boyhood, spurning her grave-clothes" (169). This resurrection recalls not so much the raising of Lazarus as it does another passage in the Fourth Gospel: " 'Truly, truly, I say to you, unless a grain of wheat falls into the earth and dies, it remains alone; but if it dies, it bears much fruit' " (12:24). Stephen certainly sees his discipleship to Daedalus as life-giving and fruit-bearing.

The reader is also influenced in his judgment on Stephen by the latter's use of the images (or symbols) of the hawk (or eagle) and the bat. Stephen, like his namesake, is hawk-like, and in his vision of the sunward-soaring artificer he reads "a prophecy of the end he had been born to serve" (169); this end, this destiny, is the destiny of the artist who, from the vantage point of an eagle, can awaken the less perceptive to an awareness of their ignorant and fallen condition. Such imagery would suggest that if Stephen is no evangelist, he is at least a prophet, more confident and more presumptuous than Moses, and yet one who like Moses saw as his destiny the leadership of an enslaved people from their bondage. Stephen sees his nation to be as enslaved and blind as the Israelites in Egypt. The soul of the Irishman was batlike, "waking to the consciousness of itself in darkness and secrecy and loneliness" (183); the thoughts and desires of his race flitted "like bats, across the dark country lanes, under trees by the edges of streams and near the poolmottled bogs" (238). At the same time Stephen was steeped enough in the tradition of his Church to recognize the folly of his action, and he must have answered affirmatively his own question: "But was it for this folly that he was about to leave for ever the house of prayer and prudence into which he had been born and the order of life out of which he had come?" (225). Folly though it may have been to leave his tradition, his possession by his call was stronger than any fear of folly.

Stephen views the artist's enterprise as an inspired one, and he turns again to the imagery of the Bible and of the Church which he has forsaken in order to express his convictions of the power and glory of his calling. As the Creator brought order out of chaos, so the artist, once he has come to an understanding of the physical creation, "[tries] slowly and humbly and constantly to express, to press out again, from the gross earth or what it brings forth, from sound and shape and colour which are the prison gates of our soul, an image of the beauty we have come to understand—that is art" (206). Furthermore, he sees the artist as the true high priest, one who is commissioned to celebrate a Eucharist far more meaningful and life-giving than that celebrated by the priest of the Church—the latter is "but schooled in the discharging of a formal rite," while Stephen as artist is "a priest of eternal imagination, transmuting the daily bread of experience into the radiant body of everliving life" (221). And this indeed is the miracle, as well as the proud presumption, of the artist; this is his hawklike function, to reveal to the blind of the world the resplendent beauty of the universe. The artist is the un-churched prophet and priest, summoning the batlike soul to a knowledge of its true condition and serving the soul with those elements which are the means of new vision and new life. Stephen's self-imposed exile is not a severance of his ties with Ireland; he goes as a kind of redeemer, bent upon forging "in the smithy of [his] soul the uncreated conscience of [his] race." (253)

The reader, in seeking to understand the nature and source of Stephen's call, thus finds himself held in nice balance by the seeming contradiction between the ortho-dox teachings of the Church on the meaning of vocation and Stephen's enthusiastic and passionate surrender to his new life as artist. And if the reader turns to the orthodox view and to Stephen's view, he might also turn to Joyce's view. It is difficult to determine the author's attitude to-ward his main character's response to the call of Daedalus. What, for example, is the degree of Joyce's irony in this portrait suggestive of his own development as an artist? Keeping in mind that the novel is not a portrait of the artist but a portrait of the artist *as a young man*, of one who has not yet gained his full maturity, are we to con-clude that Joyce is ridiculing Stephen or that he takes him with real seriousness? Does he view the youthful Stephen as a pompous and arrogant fool who bears a closer rela-tionship to Icarus than to Daedalus and whose rash, sunward flight will lead to a fatal plunge into the ocean? Or are we perhaps to take the following words of Cranly to Stephen as a reflection of Joyce's own sentiment?

> . . . you need not look upon yourself as driven away if you do not wish to go or as a heretic or an outlaw. There are many good believers who think as you do. Would that surprise you? The church is not the stone building nor even the clergy and their dogmas. It is the whole mass of those born into it. (245-246)

It is evident that a reader's final response to Stephen will be formed through a combination of many factors and that no two readers are likely to respond in exactly the same way. It seems to me that the concluding portrait is that of one who takes himself with too unadulterated a seriousness; who is too self-conscious a martyr (his Christian name may suggest to him the martyred Stephen); who, as he sees his function perilously close to the function of God, borders on the sin of *hubris* (that pride which leads man to try to play God); and who fashions some rather grandiose plans for the salvation of his nation.

It would, of course, be foolish to argue that Stephen is Christian, since he neither accepts his place gratefully as a member of Christ's Body nor points to Christ as the Way of salvation. Yet, would it not be short-sighted of the Christian to overlook the measure of Stephen's service? He may be as foreign to the communion of the Church as was the pagan Daedalus himself, yet the passion with which he embraces his calling puts to shame the lethargic and mechanical lifelessness with which such a priest as the dean of studies (185-189) responds to his call. Stephen, cut

off from the Church Visible and the nation visible, yet
serves Christian and Irishman alike as he stands in the ante-
room to salvation, fashioning those words which will call
men to a knowledge of themselves and of their place in a
mysterious and beautiful creation.

2.

THE THEME OF THE FALL:

Albert Camus' *The Fall*

> *Some were dreadfully insulted, and quite seriously,*
> *to have held up as a model such an immoral character as*
> A Hero of Our Time; *others shrewdly noticed that the*
> *author had portrayed himself and his acquaintances. . . .*
> A Hero of Our Time, *gentlemen, is in fact a portrait,*
> *but not of an individual; it is the aggregate of the vices*
> *of our whole generation in their fullest expression.* LER-
> MONTOV (Prefatory sentences to *The Fall*)*

Jean-Baptiste Clamence, narrator of Albert Camus' *The Fall*, has lived his early adult years in what to him was a state of Eden. A man of incalculable natural endowments, one of the most esteemed and revered lawyers in Paris, he has felt in complete harmony with life. His every relationship to the various aspects of physical existence, his sense of rapport with all whom he met, has been so easy and satisfying as to lead him to believe that he was born to a command of life, knowing its intricacies and complexities, needing no guide beyond his own unerring instincts. He favors his companion with a recital of the manifold quali-

---

* In this chapter, all excerpts from *The Fall* by Albert Camus are used by the permission of the publisher, Alfred A. Knopf, Inc., New York. Page references are to the Alfred A. Knopf edition, 1957, translated by Justin O'Brien.

ties and achievements of his youth—popularity, good looks, adeptness at dancing, learning, skill in courtship, justice, capabilities as athlete and art critic; fear of being thought immodest alone prevents him from indulging in a more lengthy and impressive catalogue.

To the outward eye at least, he has been the heaven-sent Patron and Protector of Justice to the widows and orphans of Paris. He has sought neither wealth nor the outward evidences of personal fame, having taken a particular delight in charity cases as long as they were noble, and having two or three times refused to accept the proffered Legion of Honor. A paragon of thoughtfulness and courtesy, he has diligently sought every conceivable opportunity for the doing of the good deed—the leading of the blind across the street, the giving of directions to the lost, the joyful distributing of alms, the continual maintaining of a watchful eye so that he might distribute his kindnesses wherever and whenever there was need. And all these things he has done expecting nothing, at least nothing of a material sort, in return. Where virtue is its own reward, what more can be sought?

This was Eden, the freedom to give rather than to receive, the freedom to judge rather than be judged, the sense of physical well-being and of the blessed possession of virtue. But on one pleasant autumn evening, Clamence goes on to tell his silent drinking companion at the *Mexico City* bar in Amsterdam, as he was contentedly looking out over the Seine from the deserted Pont des Arts, he heard a burst of laughter behind him. There was no one on the bridge, no barge or boat on the river below. The laughter, its author unseen, seemed to move downstream, and the disconcerted Clamence felt a rapid beating of his heart and a difficulty in breathing. Home again, he went to his bathroom for a drink of water and, looking in the mirror, noted that the confident smile which he had carried through his noble life was a double smile. He had fallen from Eden into hell, the circles of which bear so startling a resemblance to the concentric canals of Amsterdam.

Clamence's fall had really taken place two or three years before this episode on the Pont des Arts, but gifted as he was with the ability to forget the unpleasant, he had succeeded in keeping out of his mind the memory of his "essential discovery" (69). On that former evening, returning home from the solacing bed of a mistress, he had passed by a young woman leaning over the railing of the Pont Royal. When he had proceeded fifty yards beyond the bridge, he heard a body strike the water and heard a repeated cry going downstream. A momentary impulse to turn back was conveniently quelled by the thought, "Too late, too far . . ." (70), and Clamence returned home, keeping his secret and being careful not to read the papers for the next few days. For a while, he lived in the luxury of forgetfulness.

Had the tenacity of memory not overpowered the will to forgetfulness, Clamence might never have left the Eden of Paris and his noble defense of noble cases, might never have reached the hell-like concentric canals of Amsterdam. One example of the destructive quality of memory will suffice. The honking of Parisian horns behind Clamence one day as he was slow in responding to a green light brought back into his mind a nightmarish incident which had been covered by comforting forgetfulness. He recalled the time when a motorcycle had pulled in front of his car as he awaited the change of light. The cycle stalled, several polite requests to the cyclist to move aside were answered with increasing hostility and discourtesy, and horns were honked to the rear. Finally, the cyclist challenged Clamence to a try at fisticuffs, and as Clamence moved forward to oblige him, a stranger stepped from the curb, called the lawyer a coward, and boxed him on the ear. By that time the cyclist was off, and the honking of horns summoned Clamence from his considered retaliation of his assailant back to his car. As he drove off, his attacker humiliated him further by addressing him as "poor dope." (53)

His recollection of the episode was shattering. The noble figure of the Parisian lawyer had been humiliated in public; his dream of himself as one who would have felled his assailant and then gone on to demolish the cyclist had simply not stood up to the facts of the case, and he was no longer able to view himself as he had in his days of Eden. Not only did his memory show him to be something less than the poised, courageous, and muscular man that he thought himself; perhaps worse, it had shown him also that he was not the exemplar of justice which he had assumed himself to be:

> I learned . . . that I was on the side of the guilty, the accused, only in exactly so far as their crime caused me no harm. Their guilt made me eloquent because I was not its victim. When I was threatened, I became not only a judge in turn but even more: an irascible master who

wanted, regardless of all laws, to strike down the offender and get him on his knees. After that, *mon cher compatriote*, it is very hard to continue seriously believing one has a vocation for justice and is the predestined defender of the widow and orphan. (55-56)

The sound of the body striking the water, the epithet "poor dope," the laughter resounding in his ears, the double smile in the bathroom mirror—these called him from Eden to hell; these were the materials out of which his fall was fashioned. From the clear heights of Eden he had been called to the fog-bound, low-lying city of Amsterdam, the microcosm of hell. And what is hell? It is to know yourself, and to be known, as you really are. Hell is the revelation of the true being, the carrying of identifying visiting cards which may read

Dupont, jittery philosopher, or Christian landowner, or adulterous humanist—indeed, there's a wide choice. But it would be hell! Yes, hell must be like that: streets filled with shop signs and no way of explaining one-self. One is classified once and for all. (47)

Clamence's fall was effected through memory of his actions and motives, a memory which led him to an awareness of his pervasive and controlling characteristic: self-love. All other persons in his universe served but one purpose—to bolster his love of self. He knew nothing of friendship, nor did he want to, for friendship was a mutual, two-way relationship, a binding affection which called for a sense of obligation on both sides. He was never so capable of loving his acquaintances as at their death, for their convenient action relieved him forever of any obligation to them. His ego had constantly to be fed by his sense of domination over others, and domination necessarily calls for a master-slave relationship, rather than one in which two persons enjoy a mutual appreciation of each other's being. Clamence never sought a person with whom he could share the experience of a rich life; he looked "merely for objects of pleasure and conquest" (58), for those upon whom and through whom he could assert his own being. One of the delights of debauchery, he had discovered, was that it created no obligation; better than this, debauchery conferred a sense of immortality, draining one of memory, pain, desire, and hope, and giving one the sense of an eternal nothingness.

His fall did not involve a change of being, a metamorphosis from a lawyer motivated by the highest ideals to a degenerate who sought only his own pleasure. Rather, his fall was the transition from his mistaken conception of himself as a noble man to his knowledge of himself as a complete and ruthless egoist. Shortly after the episode of the disconcerting laughter on the bridge, he caught himself tipping his hat to a blind man after he had helped him across the street. Not until after his fall did he realize that he had always done so and that his seeming courtesy was simply designed to catch the public eye, to convince the world that Jean-Baptiste Clamence was a man of rare thoughtfulness and tender sensibilities. He defines his disease of self-love, of a passion for absolute domination over all other people, with a fine precision:

> . . . I could live happily only on condition that all the individuals on earth, or the greatest possible number,

> were turned toward me, eternally in suspense, devoid of
> independent life and ready to answer my call at any mo-
> ment, doomed in short to sterility until the day I should
> deign to favor them. In short, for me to live happily it
> was essential for the creatures I chose not to live at all.
> They must receive their life, sporadically, only at my bid-
> ding. (68)

The human condition, Clamence avers, has always been so, and the primates shared the murderous disposition which the cultured narrator now knows to be his own. But the primates were more honest and more direct; they had no ulterior motives, since their motives and their actions were all of one piece. The Dutch, less sophisticated than the French, also show something of this primitive sim- plicity. They are not above indulging in murder, and they use the proper weapon—knife or revolver. But the more civilized of our time, Clamence continues with acute irony, "kill in the bosom of the family by attrition"; they (or we) are subtly organized for murder, are like "those tiny fish in the rivers of Brazil that attack the unwary swim- mer by thousands and with swift little nibbles clean him up in a few minutes, leaving only an immaculate skeleton" (7). And as Clamence and his silent companion pass a former slave shop in the streets of Amsterdam, they note the identifying two heads of Negro slaves perched aloft. How scandalous this is to the contemporary heart which indignantly denounces the obvious slavery of yesterday and now prefers to practice its slavery in the home or in the factory! We cannot live without slavery, and yet we can- not admit our addiction to it; we must throw away our shop signs and our calling cards and practice duplicity. With all our sophistication—our use of the subjunctive, our silk underwear, our manicured nails, our knowledge of Dante—we maintain our basically destructive dispositions; our elegantly precise and modulated speech serves only to conceal our murderous hearts: ". . . style, like sheer silk, too often hides eczema" (6). A premium is placed on duplicity, on two-facedness. Clamence is bitterly aware of his true shop sign and calling card: "a double face, a charming Janus, and above it the motto of the house: 'Don't rely on it.' On my cards: 'Jean-Baptiste Clamence, play actor.'" (47)

Clamence's discovery that he has always scorned other people, has always used them as objects for his own advantage, and has always passed judgment upon them leads him to an overwhelming determination that the tables must never be turned. He must never become an object of judgment to other people. To Clamence, the evidence of such judgment was the laughter he heard on the bridge, and he has set himself to the task of eluding the laughing, scornful, and judging eyes of others. The manner through which he attempts to escape the status of object lies in the novel itself, for the novel is his confession, and his confession is, paradoxically, the very means of preventing eyes eager to judge from becoming concentrated on him. His confession serves the purpose of "silencing the laughter, of avoiding judgment personally" (131). It does so by condemning everyone, for each hearer can read in the confession his own predicament, and his attention is slowly won from concentration on Clamence to concentration on himself.

Clamence gains the right to judge others by judging himself first. He persuades his hearers of their kinship in depravity and then convinces them that his knowledge of their common state gives him an advantage over them. He then subtly removes himself from being an object of their judgment, freeing himself from their eyes and reigning over them like God the Father at the Last Judgment. (143)

Clamence confesses that he has solved his problem by accepting duplicity. He accepts the condition of slavery under the pretence that it is freedom; he would have removed the slaves' heads from the front of the shop but followed a business-as-usual policy inside the shop. He had learned that he was afraid of freedom on one evening long ago as he paid no heed to the drowning cries of a young lady in the Seine. True freedom is the courage to do the gracious and lovely action unseen by human eye, unjudged by one's fellows, and it is the courage to do so regardless of the consequences; slavery is to play to the gallery, to seek to impress human judges. Freedom is accomplished in solitude, in the face of oneself; slavery is the cowering to the judgment of society, is infidelity to the call of the innermost heart. Man, however, is far more fearful of the judgment of others than he is of judgment of self. Since man will judge and since there can be no basis for man's judgment of man without laws, without a code of behavior against which man can be judged, a legal system is called for; and since God is out of style, the society of man must construct its own code, replete with enough punishments to satisfy man that he is paying for his sins—and drained of any concept of grace. Law and judgment without grace is prophecy without redemption, and Clamence has bowed to this hell which man has created:

> In solitude and when fatigued, one is after all inclined to take oneself for a prophet. When all is said and done, that's really what I am, having taken refuge in a desert of stones, fogs, and stagnant waters—an empty prophet for shabby times, Elijah without a messiah, choked with fever and alcohol, my back up against this moldy door, my finger raised toward a threatening sky, showering imprecations on lawless men who cannot endure any judgment. For they can't endure it, *très cher*, and that's the whole question. He who clings to a law does not fear the judgment that reinstates him in an order he believes in. But the keenest of human torments is to be judged without a law. Yet we are in that torment. Deprived of their natural curb, the judges, loosed at random, are racing through their job. Hence we have to try to go faster than they, don't we? And it's a real madhouse. Prophets and quacks multiply; they hasten to get there with a good law or a flawless organization before the world is deserted. Fortunately, *I* arrived! I am the end and the beginning; I announce the law. In short, I am a judge-penitent. (117-118)

But self-accusation is not enough to free oneself from guilt. Salvation comes at a higher price. Perhaps, if the young woman would throw herself once again into the water, there would be chance for redemption. "But," Clamence concludes, "let's not worry! It's too late now. It will always be too late. Fortunately!" (147)

II

Most Christians have formed their interpretation of the fall of man through the narrative of the third chapter of

Genesis and its gloss in the fifth chapter of Romans; those who have endured or enjoyed a course in Sophomore English have a variety of fanciful elaborations on the story through their exposure to Milton. In the Genesis account Eve, tempted by the serpent, eats the fruit of a tree from which God has forbidden her to eat upon penalty of death. Pleased with the fruit, she shares it with her husband. God summons them and pronounces his punishments upon the serpent, Eve, and Adam. Adam is driven from the garden in the company of Eve. The books of the Old Testament and the four Gospels are, among other things, the continued story of man as sinner but give no indication of any causal relationship between the sin of Adam and Eve and that of their extensive progeny.

It would be impossible to overemphasize Paul's influence on the Christian view of the fall. In the Old Testament there is no trace (one might argue a possible exception in Psalm 51:5) of what we have come to call the doctrine of original sin, though there is rather considerable evidence that sin is universal. Paul's interpretation of the causal relationship between the sin of Adam and the sin of mankind is not original with him; it is found in Jesus ben Sirach's Apocryphal book of Ecclesiasticus. But few Christians read the Old Testament Apocrypha which, in any case, do not carry the same weight as the canonical books of the Bible. Paul, with ample latter-day assistance from Augustine, Luther, and Calvin, has the glory or shame of responsibility for one of the central doctrines of the Christian tradition—the doctrine of original sin.

According to this view, a historical Adam acted as representative for all mankind, sinning not only in his own person but also for every man. With each human conception, the sin that was in Adam's loins is transmitted seminally: we are conceived in sin and born sinners. The doctrine is based in part on the concept of the solidarity of mankind, of the close relationship and interdependence among all men. Directly linked to the fact of sin is the fact of death, in accordance with the Lord's admonition to Adam: ". . . in the day that you eat of it you shall die" (Genesis 2:17). The most explicit statements of the doctrine are found in the fifth chapter of Romans: "Therefore as sin came into the world through one man and death through sin. . . ." "If, because of one man's trespass, death reigned through that one man. . . ." "Then as one man's trespass led to condemnation for all men. . . ." It is of greatest importance to note that these clauses do not simply affirm the rather self-evident fact, one easily noted on the basis of empirical observation, that all men are sinners. They affirm that the ineradicable and indefatigable disposition to sin is built-in, standard equipment of every human being and is destined to be so because of his common inheritance from one who sinned in behalf of all of us, Adam. It is not a matter of choice, not a local option, not a temptation that must be fallen to anew; it is a once-and-for-all action, Adam's action.

In the hands of the early Church Fathers, there was a proliferation of the doctrine, culminating in the writings of Augustine, incalculably the greatest influence on the Protestant tradition between Paul and Luther. The two principal addenda were the doctrines of original righteousness or perfection and of original guilt. The former attests to what a cataclysmic tragedy Adam's fall actually was, picturing Adam's innocent state as one of inexpressible righteousness and perfection—a view which Milton endorses in lovely and stately rhythm. The emphasis is on what man lost through Adam's defection. Interestingly enough, the biblical passage most suggestive of original perfection is found not in any description of Adam before his fall, but in Ezekiel's lamentation over the king of Tyre:

> "You were the signet of perfection,
>> full of wisdom
>> and perfect in beauty.
> You were in Eden, the garden of God;
>> every precious stone was your covering,
> carnelian, topaz, and jasper,
>> chrysolite, beryl, and onyx,
> sapphire, carbuncle, and emerald;
>> and wrought in gold were your settings
>> and your engravings.
> On the day that you were created
>> they were prepared.
> With an anointed guardian cherub I placed you;
>> you were on the holy mountain of God;
>> in the midst of the stones of fire you walked.
> You were blameless in your ways
>> from the day you were created,
>> till iniquity was found in you.
> In the abundance of your trade
>> you were filled with violence, and you sinned;
> so I cast you as a profane thing from the mountain of God,
>> and the guardian cherub drove you out
>> from the midst of the stones of fire.

Your heart was proud because of your beauty;
      you corrupted your wisdom for the sake of your
      splendor." (28:12-17)

The doctrine of original guilt finds every man not only sinful but also guilty: man is not only affected by Adam's sin, is not simply the unfortunate victim of an act beyond his control; he is also responsible for it, is viewed as an active participant in the eating of the fruit.

The Pauline interpretation of the fall and of sin, carried on in essence by such influential figures as Augustine, Luther, and Calvin, is the more orthodox, conservative, and literal one. It was unquestionably the dominant view of Christendom until well into the nineteenth century. Contending with it since that time is another interpretation of the Genesis narrative, a view proceeding from the belief that the third chapter of Genesis is to be read as myth rather than as a literal account of a historical event. Its premise is that God reveals himself to man through Scripture in a variety of ways, and that just as the parables of Jesus are designed to show man the nature of the human condition through dramatic narrative rather than through incidents of fact, so are some of the passages of the Old Testament designed to show the eternal nature of man's relationship to God through myth rather than through historical occurrences. A myth is not a fanciful, extravagant tale spun out of the cloth of man's imagination; it is a revealed truth, an explanation of some perplexing problem which faces man. To this school of thought Adam, which in Hebrew means "man," is Everyman, and Adam's fall is one re-enacted by each human being. The fall narrative is thus viewed as revealing the nature of every man as sinner, the nature of God as Creator of one born good but free to fall, and the nature of the relationship between sinful man and the judging and merciful God.

But from whichever of these two vantage points one reads the third chapter of Genesis, the interpretation of man's "prelapsarian" (before the fall) state, and of the cause, nature, and results of sin remain in most respects the same. There is within the Christian faith no disputing the fact that "God saw everything that he had made, and behold, it was very good" (Genesis 1:31), and there is no disputing the fact that man, whether or not he is descended from a historical Adam, has fallen from a state of grace.

In the biblical view the fall was occasioned by two closely related qualities, pride and idolatry, the principal ingredients of sin. It was too much for Eve when the serpent told her that if she ate the fruit, she would be like God. The irony is manifold. In the first place, man should indeed yearn to be like God, but the path to this kind of righteousness is a submission to God's will, not a defiance of it. Second, Eve did in a sense become like God in that she decided to give her foremost allegiance to her own will and judgment, thus becoming the object of her own worship, a god to herself. Finally, however, Eve was to learn of her bad bargain, discovering that her new sovereign was a most frail substitute for Jahweh. Eve's pride led to self-idolatry; Isaiah might have taunted her as he did the king of Babylon:

> You said in your heart,
> "I will ascend to heaven;

above the stars of God
    I will set my throne on high;
I will sit on the mount of assembly
    in the far north;
I will ascend above the heights of the clouds,
    I will make myself like the Most High."
But you are brought down to Sheol,
    to the depths of the Pit. (14:13-15)

Pride inevitably leads to some kind of idolatry, that is, the focusing of one's worship, one's ultimate fidelity, on someone or something other than the One God. Such is the burden of the first chapter of Romans. God's wrath was evoked because men, "claiming to be wise, . . . became fools, and exchanged the glory of the immortal God for images resembling mortal man or birds or animals or reptiles," because men "exchanged the truth about God for a lie and worshiped and served the creature rather than the Creator. . . ." When man so chooses any master other than God, the Lord will give him up to the consequences of his choice. Paul amasses an impressive catalogue of those qualities which will oppress the idolator, including envy, a disposition to murder, deceit, malignity, slander, insolence, haughtiness, boastfulness, disobedience, faithlessness, ruthlessness. And the more poetic Isaiah pronounces upon Judah the wrath which has followed upon their rebellion from Jahweh:

Ah, sinful nation,
    a people laden with iniquity,
offspring of evildoers,
    sons who deal corruptly!

> They have forsaken the Lord,
>   they have despised the Holy One of Israel,
>   they are utterly estranged.
> Why will you still be smitten,
>   that you continue to rebel?
> The whole head is sick,
>   and the whole heart faint.
> From the sole of the foot even to the head,
>   there is no soundness in it,
> but bruises and sores
>   and bleeding wounds;
> they are not pressed out, or bound up,
>   or softened with oil. (1:4-6)

The essence of the biblical revelation on the fall is that man was created good and free; that he abused his freedom, falling to the temptation of pride, which in turn led to some form of idolatry; and that he was given up by God to the bitter fruits of his idolatry and thus lived estranged from the only source of life and goodness. But the biblical message does not end on this despairing note, for if, as Paul writes in the first chapter of Romans, the Lord is willing to deliver the idolatrous man over to the bondage of his sins, He does not forget him. In recalling the fact that Jahweh pronounced judgment upon Adam and Eve after the eating of the fruit, it is well to recall also that Jahweh returned to the Garden and spoke to them, and that he has been speaking to man often since. Man's despair would be God walking in the other direction, a nightmarish vision of an eternal departure rather than an eternal approach, a welcome approach even if it carries with it the fearful prophetic voice pronouncing judgment upon us for our sins. For judgment is never an end in itself; it is a means of awakening the human spirit to a consciousness of its own depravity so that it may seek its strength elsewhere; it is a prelude to repentance; and justice carries with itself a perfect balance—mercy. Through the Old Testament prophets, God continues to call man away from his multiplicity of false gods and back to a worship of Himself. Abraham, Moses, David, Isaiah, Jeremiah, Ezekiel, and others, each in his own way, serve as Jahweh's instruments to reach the heart of man.

The culmination of God's reconciling activity is found in the incarnation and cross of Jesus Christ and in the continuing work of the Holy Spirit. Paul juxtaposes Adam and Christ, showing antithetically how Christ, the second Adam, was the means of reconciling man to God from whom the first Adam had sundered him.

> Then as one man's trespass led to condemnation for all men, so one man's act of righteousness leads to acquittal and life for all men. For as by one man's disobedience many were made sinners, so by one man's obedience many will be made righteous. (Romans 5:18-19)

This is a Paradise Lost—Paradise Regained motif in which the disobedience of Adam is countered by the obedience of Christ. Man, who had served Satan and worked wickedness through Adam, could now return to God through Christ. God, by an act of love—the sacrifice of his Son to the blood of the cross—reconciled man to Himself, and the reconciliation freed man from his bondage to idolatry. Man's heart, turned from pride and idolatry, was now free to love God and neighbor. When man receives this gift of love, he is redeemed from the grievous effects of the fall: he has been born anew.

III

There is an important distinction between the biblical doctrine of the fall and Jean-Baptiste Clamence's concept of his own fall. The innocence of Adam and Eve was a state of sinlessness; their fall was a disobedient succumbing to the sins of pride and idolatry. The innocence of Clamence was a state of unawareness of his sin; his fall from innocence was a gradual recognition of the fact that he had been a sinner without knowing it. Clamence's fall was more clearly a coming to a knowledge of good and evil than was Adam's, for Clamence had mistaken evil for good until he fell; his fall is actually a conviction of sin, an intellectual awareness of what really distinguishes the evil from the good. His fall frees him from self-righteousness, though not from unrighteousness.

Clamence's discovery was that his actions belied his motives, that the appearance of his outer self and the reality of his inner self bore no relationship. When he spoke of himself as "a double face, a charming Janus," he spoke with a penetrating accuracy. His discovery was the same as that of T. S. Eliot's Thomas Becket when he was confronted by the Fourth Tempter in *Murder in the Cathedral:* he was doing the right deed for the wrong reason. By delving into his memory, Clamence realized that "modesty helped me to shine, humility to conquer, and virtue to oppress" (84), that "the surface of all my virtues had a less imposing reverse side" (85). His every noble and helpful action before his fall had been motivated by his passion to feel above others, to take his stance on some summit, "well above the human ants" (24). His legal profession and success served perfectly to sustain his sense of freedom and superiority:

> My profession satisfied most happily that vocation for summits. It cleansed me of all bitterness toward my neighbor, whom I always obligated without ever owing him anything. It set me above the judge whom I judged in turn, above the defendant whom I forced to gratitude. Just weigh this, *cher monsieur*, I lived with impunity. I was concerned in no judgment; I was not on the floor of the courtroom, but somewhere in the flies like those gods that are brought down by machinery from time to time to transfigure the action and give it its meaning. After all, living aloft is still the only way of being seen and hailed by the largest number. (25)

The theologian who has given us the deepest insight into the nature of the sin which possesses Clamence and the rest of us is Martin Buber, whose influence on contemporary theology and literature, particularly through his essay entitled *I and Thou*, has been tremendous. One of the most interesting literary examples of Professor Buber's thesis— that there are two principal kinds of relationship which may exist between two beings, an "I-it" relationship and an "I-thou" relationship—is Eliot's *The Cocktail Party*. At the beginning of the play Edward Chamberlayne and his wife, Lavinia, respond to each other as if the other were an inanimate object, an it, rather than a human being. A person's response to an inanimate object is one of domination; such an "I-it" (or person-object) situation makes for a master-slave relationship which is quite foreign to any proper interpersonal relationship. A person views his typewriter, for example, as an object made to serve him; he simply *uses* the typewriter, paying little regard to its feelings and making no strenuous effort to enter into a dialogue with it. A man's relation to his typewriter is that of an I to an it. Of a similar nature is Edward's relationship to Lavinia. It is true that he gives her many evidences of outward respect, but such consideration springs not from his sense of the dignity of her person or from any love he bears her, but simply from the fact that such action makes him think well of himself, enables him to view himself as a model husband. He thus uses her as an object to bolster his own ego. Lavinia is similarly motivated; she wishes Edward to be a successful lawyer not because of any pride she has in him or any concern she has for his person, but because she desires the prestige and wealth which will come to the wife of such a man. Knowing each other only as objects and not as persons, they feel estranged and alienated, for there is no communication between objects or between a person and an object. As they learn in the course of the play, people can come to know each other only as they agree to encounter each other as persons, as they enter into some kind of participation, as they experience some kind of oneness even while keeping their own identities.

Clamence is a perfect example of a person whose love of self is so complete that there is no room for other persons in his closed universe: "It is not true, after all, that I never loved. I conceived at least one great love in my life, of which I was always the object. . . . I looked merely for objects of pleasure and conquest" (58). "To be happy," he asserts, "it is essential not to be too concerned with others" (80). But the more he struggles for happiness and freedom, the more he becomes trapped in that hell of isolation and self-love. He lives in the most pretentious of all worlds, a world in which there exist only one person and many objects. The one person of Clamence's world is Clamence; all other human beings become for him objects to be used and manipulated for his own self-gratification. It is no wonder that he eschews friendships, for they are binding, calling for mutual obligations; it is little wonder either that he loves his acquaintances most upon their death, for death ends any possible claim which they may place upon him. His fall is the discovery that his world has always been one of "I-it" relationships.

In Christian thought a conviction of sin is an essential part of the process of redemption. By means of his vision of God through Christ the Christian becomes shockingly aware of that vast distinction between the Godhead and his own depraved and unhealthy state. His conviction is his knowledge that he has loved neither God nor neighbor, that he has, like Clamence, loved himself to the exclusion of all others. The vision is so stunning and gracious that it not only convicts him of sin but draws him toward itself, serving as a means to lead him from unrighteousness or self-righteousness to righteousness. The Christian is foreshadowed in the publican who knew of both his sin and his salvation: "God, be merciful to me a sinner!" (Luke 18:13)

Clamence is convicted of his sin but remains uncertain

of the way to redemption; in fact, he is by no means certain that there is a way. He does have some impulse toward truth, toward showing himself as he really is, not simply to his cultured companion in Amsterdam, but to the fortunate beneficiaries of his selfishly motivated actions as well. He feels called upon to make known his duplicity: to jostle the blind, toward whom he really feels a degree of loathing, and to slap infants. Though he never went so far as this, he did ease his conscience by complaining to the proprietor of a sidewalk restaurant about a beggar who approached him while he was eating. And he did suggest in a lecture to a group of young lawyers that he was far more wicked than some murderer whom he might defend in court. But these overtures to truth were motivated not so much by an abstract love of truth as by a desire to escape the laughter and judgment of mankind. He sought to perfect his self-accusation not as a step toward Christian redemption, but as a means of maintaining his advantage over his fellow men:

> You see, it is not enough to accuse yourself in order to clear yourself; otherwise, I'd be as innocent as a lamb. One must accuse oneself in a certain way, which it took me considerable time to perfect. I did not discover it until I fell into the most utterly forlorn state. Until then, the laughter continued to drift my way, without my random efforts succeeding in divesting it of its benevolent, almost tender quality that hurt me. (95-96)

Ironically, Clamence, seeking freedom, was instead making himself the perfect slave of mankind. Deaf to God's judgment, he lent his ear only to the judgment of men.

Paul's question to the Galatians might very appropriately have been put to him: "Am I now seeking the favor of men, or of God? Or am I trying to please men?" (1:10). Paul's counsel to the Romans would also have a fine appropriateness: "Do not be conformed to this world but be transformed by the renewal of your mind, that you may prove what is the will of God, what is good and acceptable and perfect." (12:2)

Finally, does Clamence leave us with the belief that he is eternally damned to the concentric circles of hell so adequately suggested by the canal-imposed structure of Amsterdam? Is he to be forever enslaved in that last circle reserved for traitors to God? Is he to remain always touched by "the breath of stagnant waters, the smell of dead leaves soaking in the canal and the funereal scent rising from the barges loaded with flowers" (43)? Are we to accept his closing words that the chance for salvation is past?—"It's too late now. It will always be too late. Fortunately!" (147)

Possibly so, and yet one must ask several questions. How are we to account for the facts that the narrator has adopted the name of Jean-Baptiste or John the Baptist, that the waters near Amsterdam are referred to as an "immense holy-water font" (109), and that doves (traditional symbols of the Holy Spirit) are always hovering above the fog of the city? Has Camus placed Clamence in Amsterdam simply because it is a mecca for the kinds of persons who enable him successfully to ply his profession as judge-penitent, or because it suggests a wilderness awaiting a Messiah?

While traveling with his companion on the Zuider Zee,

Clamence recalls that day aboard the upper deck of an ocean liner when his sighting of a black speck on the ocean horrified him, reminding him of a body in the Seine some years before and the cry of a drowning woman. He realized that that cry, that conviction of his sin,

> had never ceased, carried by the river to the waters of the Channel, to travel throughout the world, across the limitless expanse of the ocean, and that it had waited for me there [on the liner] until the day I had encountered it. I realized likewise that it would continue to await me on seas and rivers, everywhere, in short, where lies the bitter water of my baptism. Here, too, by the way, aren't we on the water? . . . We shall never get out of this immense holy-water font. (108-109)

Clamence, convinced of his sin and surrounded by baptismal water, is also aware of the doves flapping above Amsterdam and waiting to descend: "The doves wait up there all year round. They wheel above the earth, look down, and would like to come down. But there is nothing but the sea and the canals, roofs covered with shop signs, and never a head on which to light" (73). The prophet, the water, the doves are all present; only a Messiah is missing, the Christ at whose baptism the dove descended, alighting upon him. And what are we to make of Clamence's wandering and confused vision toward the end of his confession where the huge snowflakes approximate to him the descent of the doves, possibly the bearers of the good news, the messengers of salvation? Is Clamence to remain "a false prophet crying in the wilderness and refusing to come forth" (147), or is he to answer his call as John the Baptist, also a voice in the wilderness, but a voice whose conviction of sin leads him to

cry, " 'Repent, for the kingdom of heaven is at hand' "
(Matthew 3:2)?

These are questions for us to ponder in this confession of
a midtwentieth-century Mr. Anthropos to his cultured
contemporaries, to you and to me; for the confessor is, as
Camus suggests in his prefatory sentences from Lermontov,
*"the aggregate of the vices of our whole generation in their
fullest expression."* And the ear which attends Clamence in
the *Mexico City* bar and in the streets of Amsterdam and
its environs is the ear of the educated, and presumably secular, man of our time, a time in which man exhibits only
"two passions: ideas and fornication" (6), and in which
he has no serious commitments, doing all things only " 'in
a way' " (8). The confession is made to one who, despite
his familiarity with the subjunctive, his knowledge of the
Bible and Dante and the Orient, nevertheless fails to understand the symbolic references to doves (73) and does not
recognize van Eyck's painting of "The Just Judges." (128)

One's interpretation of the novel must rest ultimately on
his judgment of its irony. Clamence, it would seem, is a
supreme ironist who uses the images and symbols of the
Christian faith finally to imply their meaninglessness to and
emptiness for him and his generation. Clamence, it seems,
sees or is aware of no hope. He feels that if faced again
with a young woman's plunge from a bridge, he would
repeat his cowardly withdrawal. But one can not with cer-
tainty equate the author's point of view with the narrator's, and in *The Fall* there may be irony within irony.
Perhaps Camus is ironically implying that Clamence, not
knowing himself as well as he thinks he does, has courage-

ously made an agonizing descent into the lower depths and
has been shattered to the point at which the Holy Spirit
may claim his soul. In this matter each reader's own
sensitivity must be his guide, for the artist is not called
upon to furnish the kind of explicit resolution which may
characterize theological exposition.

3.

THE THEME OF JUDGMENT:

Franz Kafka's *The Trial*

Wretched man that I am! Who will deliver me from this body of death? (Romans 7:24)

I

"It is Justice," said the painter at last. "Now I can recognize it," said K. "There's the bandage over the eyes, and here are the scales. But aren't there wings on the figure's heels, and isn't it flying?" "Yes," said the painter, "my instructions were to paint it like that; actually it is Justice and the goddess of Victory in one." "Not a very good combination, surely," said K., smiling. "Justice must stand quite still, or else the scales will waver and a just verdict will become impossible." "I had to follow my client's instructions," said the painter. (182-183)*

In the world of Joseph K., central figure of Franz Kafka's *The Trial*, justice is as elusive as it is in the painting of Titorelli, with whom K. is talking in the dialogue above. And the meaning of the novel itself seems at times as elusive to its reader as Justice is to K. The problem of the

---

* In this chapter, all excerpts from *The Trial* by Franz Kafka are used by the permission of the publisher, Alfred A. Knopf, Inc., New York. Page references are to the Definitive Edition, 1957, translated by Willa and Edwin Muir.

reader is like that of the person who, owning one of those small, circular, glass-topped boxes containing three metal pellets and three holes, tries to capture the three pellets simultaneously in the three holes. He will succeed in arresting two of them, but his effort to arrest the third will result in the other two rolling from their fixed positions; in frustration he will wish to smash the glass top and finger the pellets into the holes. The glass top of *The Trial* is smash-proof, and it is the rare, perhaps even nonexistent, reader who can understand all parts of the novel in such a way that they fit together under any single, all-inclusive interpretation.

The novel calls to mind various other great literary works. Like the Book of Job it is an anguished cry for justice, but it does not present the voice of the Lord answering out of the whirlwind and is consequently less conclusive than Job. Like *The Pilgrim's Progress* it is a kind of dream allegory, but Bunyan's dream bears a step-by-step resemblance to a readily familiar Christian doctrine, whereas K.'s nightmare bears a resemblance to a human condition the nature of which is far more impenetrable than the dogmas of Christian faith. Like *Alice in Wonderland* it offers a world of fantasy and surprise, but it calls more urgently than Lewis Carroll's book for a translation of its events and characters into the events and characters which man encounters in his pilgrimage through this real world of space and time. Yet the enigmatic quality of *The Trial*, stumbling block as it may be, is no roadblock, and though the reader will probably never rest perfectly satisfied with his interpretation of the novel, he will turn from it as the

Wedding-Guest turned from the Ancient Mariner—"a sadder and a wiser man."

Joseph K. awakes in his boarding house on the morning of his thirtieth birthday, and when the cook does not bring him his breakfast, he rings the bell. Answering the summons of the bell is not the cook but a strange man. K. learns that he is under arrest; he is not aware of any wrongdoing which might have precipitated the arrest, and the two warders who have come to his dwelling are unable to enlighten him. He is informed that the officials who have sent the warders never initiate a search for criminals; they are simply drawn toward the guilty, "as the Law decrees" (10). This is a law unfamiliar to K., and he suggests that it may be simply a fabrication of the warder's imagination. When he is questioned by a visiting Inspector he admits that he is not very much surprised by his arrest, yet he cannot recall any offense with which he might be charged. He learns that he is not to be confined but may pursue his usual business activity as Chief Clerk of a bank. He then taxis off to his work, considerably annoyed by the interruption but not disposed to take the matter with great seriousness.

The remainder of the novel, all the way to K.'s murder (or suicide), is his agonized struggle to prove his innocence or ascertain the nature of his guilt. Notwithstanding its unremitting satire on bureaucracy and its reduction to absurdity of the pretentions to justice of various courts and institutions, *The Trial* remains primarily a courageous and harrowing search for a just Redeemer, however far he may be removed from the world of history. K. learns the almost unendurable frustration of the human dichotomy—the demand to live in two worlds at once and to lend an ear to two seemingly unrelated criteria of justice. He finds, for example, that it becomes increasingly less possible to concentrate simultaneously on the outer world, represented by his commitments to the bank, and on the inner world, represented by his nightmarish call to the bar of justice. Immediately after his arrest he is surprised by the Inspector's asking him if he is not now going to the bank, and he is then assured of at least that measure of freedom: " 'You are under arrest, certainly, but that need not hinder you from going about your business' " (20). But as the case goes on and as K. becomes more and more engrossed in his search for justice, he discovers that he is very much hindered from going about his business. He becomes increasingly less able to concentrate on his banking duties, and he sees with bitter disappointment and anger that his main rival at the bank, the Assistant Manager, subsumes more and more of the responsibilities which had been K.'s and which, if successfully carried out, would lead to promotion. That K. was destined to neglect either the trial (represented by the Inspector) or his banking duties (represented by three bank clerks) is shown early in the novel: "Then K. remembered that he had not noticed the Inspector and the warders leaving, the Inspector had usurped his attention so that he did not recognize the three clerks, and the clerks in turn had made him oblivious of the Inspector." (22)

This bifurcation extends beyond his personal life and into the court system. For the normal conditions of everyday life, his country enjoyed a good legal system: "K. lived in a country with a legal constitution, there was universal peace, all the laws were in force . . ." (7). But the court to which K. is summoned (or to which he summons himself) is far removed from the civil and criminal courts of his country. It holds its sessions in the attic of a tenement house, is presided over by a thoroughly unprepossessing and dissolute magistrate, is peopled by strange human creatures who stand in bent posture under the low ceilings, and may be interrupted at any moment by the public love-making of a law student and the wife of a court usher in a corner of the room. It is not a court to which an ordinary lawyer has easy access, a fact which accounts for the arresting Inspector's surprise when K., in his early naïve state, asks permission to call his regular lawyer. Indeed, the entire trial is possessed by a nightmarish frustration, right from the first appearance of the warders. We learn that the warder Franz "overtopped K. enormously and kept clapping him on the shoulder" (6), and that "the belly of the second warder . . . kept butting against him in an almost friendly way, yet if he looked up he caught sight of a face which did not in the least suit that fat body, a dry, bony face with a great nose, twisted to one side, which seemed to be consulting over his head with the other warder" (7). K. is told by his worldly-wise Uncle Albert of an old proverb to the effect that cases like his are always lost. He learns that a defendant can never plead his case before the higher officials. And from the lawyer Huld, who specializes in cases of his kind, he hears the following dreary recital about past cases of a like nature:

> . . . it did sometimes happen that the case took a turn where the lawyer could no longer follow it. The case and

the accused and everything were simply withdrawn from the lawyer; then even the best connections with officials could no longer achieve any result, for even they knew nothing. The case had simply reached the stage where further assistance was ruled out, it was being conducted in remote, inaccessible Courts, where even the accused was beyond the reach of a lawyer. Then you might come home some day and find on your table all the countless pleas relating to the case, which you had drawn up with such pains and such flattering hopes; they had been returned to you because in the new stage of the trial they were not admitted as relevant; they were mere waste paper. It did not follow that the case was lost, by no means, at least there was no decisive evidence for such an assumption; you simply knew nothing more about the case and would never know anything more about it. (154)

There are few gambits which K. neglects in an effort to free himself from his painful predicament. He finds that he must soon surrender his first hope that the Law which harassed him was unreal, existing only in the mind of the warder. He learns quickly that he must abandon his early disposition not to take his case seriously. His proud efforts to win over the spectators at his first interrogation are humbled by failure. His looking to various women—Fräulein Bürstner; the promiscuous wife of the court usher; and the equally promiscuous Leni, nurse to lawyer Huld—for help proves worse than futile. His insistent proclamation of his innocence gains him nothing. A wiser man, if a wiser man exists, would have followed the initial advice of the Inspector: " '. . . think less about us and of what is going to happen to you, think more about yourself instead. And don't make such an outcry about your feeling innocent, it spoils the not unfavorable impression you make in other respects' " (17). If the Inspector suggests a good course of action, certainly the condition of the tradesman Block, another client of Huld, should make clear the results of a wrong approach to one's trial. For Block also is a genius in selecting blind alleys. He has under his employment a battery of five lawyers in addition to Huld; he has spent his every penny on outside help, insisting that "the only pointless thing is to try taking independent action" (219); he has assumed an abject dependence upon Leni; he has sought his salvation in the wrong place, having studied "every precept of duty, piety, and tradition" (240). His efforts and his fears have had only one result, to transform him into a pitifully groveling creature in bondage to various outside forces, particularly Huld and Leni.

K. takes a step in the right direction when he decides to assume a closer direction of his own case: "the whole of one's life would have to be recalled to mind, down to the smallest actions and accidents, clearly formulated and examined from every angle" (161). Had K. done simply that, he might have been rescued from his labyrinthine dilemma. But he goes about this not with the determination of coming to a knowledge of his real self, but with the presupposition that he is innocent and would thus establish the fact of his innocence before the Court. Recognizing at last that he must accept the trial, he nevertheless determines that he "should banish from his mind once and for all the idea of possible guilt. . . . The right tactics were to avoid letting one's thoughts stray to one's own possible shortcomings, and to cling as firmly as one could to the thought of one's advantage" (158-159). And though he is willing to dispense with the useless services of the lawyer Huld, he clings to the idea of soliciting assistance from others. Once he has drawn up his defense, "K. himself, or one of the women, or some other messenger must keep at the officials day after day. . . ." (159)

The two most revealing sections of *The Trial* are K.'s visit to the painter Titorelli in his attic studio and his unexpected meeting with the priest in the Cathedral. One of K.'s business acquaintances suggests that Titorelli may be in a position to help him in his difficult case, and K. immediately goes to the painter's studio. Titorelli tells K. that there are three different kinds of acquittal in cases like his: definite acquittal, ostensible acquittal, and indefinite postponement. A definite acquittal is granted only to the innocent and requires no intercession or influence from any outside source whatsoever. This kind of acquittal is the prerogative of the highest Court alone, a Court which, according to Titorelli, is inaccessible to everyone. The acquittal is marked by a complete annulment and destruction of all the records of the case. Titorelli has never, in his very considerable experience, met with a case of definite acquittal, but the written Law attests to the reality of such a judgment, and there are ancient legends which tell of individuals who have been so blessed. These legends, however, will exert no influence on the Court before which K. has appeared.

The other two possibilities—ostensible acquittal and indefinite postponement—fall well within the realm of Titorelli's experience. Since the Court, the one accessible to K., is deaf to any proof of innocence brought before it, the defendant must work by indirection, seeking some kind of intervention from those who have influence with the Court. The verdict of ostensible acquittal is gained by having a friend of the accused write out an affidavit of his innocence and present it directly to the Judges. With expert handling the friend can effect a decision in which the burden of the charge is removed from the defendant's shoulders, though the lower Judges do not have the power of absolving his guilt. In fact, an ostensible acquittal is only a temporary one, since the records of the case remain, continue to be circulated, and may be used at any time to summon the defendant again. Arrests may continue at frequent or infrequent intervals, and each arrest carries with it the necessity of repeating the process. An indefinite postponement is, as the name implies, even less conclusive. Such a tack prevents the case from ever getting beyond its initial stages; it preserves the defendant from the intense strain which he must endure with each new effort for an ostensible acquittal, but it demands a constant vigilance: the defendant and, to an even greater extent, his advocate must keep in constant touch with the Court. Its rigors, though less violent, are more incessant.

The atmospheric oppressiveness of the studio and the frustrating implications of the painter's remarks weigh heavily on K., and he becomes physically ill. But he does not depart before grasping the real significance of Titorelli's discourse. He notes that both ostensible acquittal and indefinite postponement serve to hold off any actual sentence upon the defendant; and he perceives, even more importantly and to his great discomfort, that "they also prevent an actual acquittal"; this observation, asserts Titorelli, is "the kernel of the matter." (202)

K.'s conversation with the priest in the Cathedral is of considerable importance. K. has gone to the Cathedral on an appointment to meet one of his bank's influential clients, an Italian who wishes a conducted tour. The Italian failing to appear, K. is just about to leave the Cathedral when a priest standing in the pulpit summons him by name and then introduces himself as the prison chaplain. Their conversation immediately turns to K.'s trial, and the priest protests that K. seeks to depend too much on outside help, the wrong kind of help. When K questions the wisdom of this advice, the priest shrieks like one observing the self-imposed doom of a fallen man, " 'Can't you see one pace before you?' " (265). K., impressed by the priest's obviously good intentions, feels that the priest may be able to advise him how to circumvent the lower Court altogether —a far wiser plan than any which involved influential manipulation of the Judges. The priest's answer, and the riddling key to K.'s problem and to the nature of his delusion, is given in the form of a parable, one which calls for full quotation:

> "In the writings which preface the Law that particular delusion is described thus: before the Law stands a doorkeeper. To this doorkeeper there comes a man from the country who begs for admittance to the Law. But the doorkeeper says that he cannot admit the man at the moment. The man, on reflection, asks if he will be allowed, then, to enter later. 'It is possible,' answers the

doorkeeper, 'but not at this moment.' Since the door leading into the Law stands open as usual and the doorkeeper steps to one side, the man bends down to peer through the entrance. When the doorkeeper sees that, he laughs and says: 'If you are so strongly tempted, try to get in without my permission. But note that I am powerful. And I am only the lowest doorkeeper. From hall to hall, keepers stand at every door, one more powerful than the other. And the sight of the third man is already more than even I can stand.' These are difficulties which the man from the country has not expected to meet, the Law, he thinks, should be accessible to every man and at all times, but when he looks more closely at the doorkeeper in his furred robe, with his huge pointed nose and long thin Tartar beard, he decides that he had better wait until he gets permission to enter. The doorkeeper gives him a stool and lets him sit down at the side of the door. There he sits waiting for days and years. He makes many attempts to be allowed in and wearies the doorkeeper with his importunity. The doorkeeper often engages him in brief conversation, asking him about his home and about other matters, but the questions are put quite impersonally, as great men put questions, and always conclude with the statement that the man cannot be allowed to enter yet. The man, who has equipped himself with many things for his journey, parts with all he has, however valuable, in the hope of bribing the doorkeeper. The doorkeeper accepts it all, saying, however, as he takes each gift: 'I take this only to keep you from feeling that you have left something undone.' During all these long years the man watches the doorkeeper almost incessantly. He forgets about the other doorkeepers, and this one seems to him the only barrier between himself and the Law. In the first years he curses his evil fate aloud; later, as he grows old, he only mutters to himself. He grows childish, and since in his prolonged study of the doorkeeper he has learned to know even the fleas in his fur collar, he begs the very fleas to help him and to persuade the doorkeeper to change his mind. Finally his eyes grow dim and he does not know whether the world is really darkening around him or whether his eyes are only deceiving him. But in the darkness he can now perceive a radiance that streams inextinguishably from the door of the Law. Now his life is drawing to a close. Before he dies, all that he has experienced during the whole time of his sojourn condenses in his mind into one question, which he has never yet put to the doorkeeper. He beckons the doorkeeper, since he can no longer raise his stiffening body. The doorkeeper has to bend far down to hear him, for the difference in size between them has increased very much to the man's disadvantage. 'What do you want to know now?' asks the doorkeeper, 'you are insatiable.' 'Everyone strives to attain the Law,' answers the man, 'how does it come about, then, that in all these years no one has come seeking admittance but me?' The doorkeeper perceives that the man is nearing his end and his hearing is failing, so he bellows in his ear: 'No one but you could gain admittance through this door, since this door was intended for you. I am now going to shut it." (267-269)

The priest's purpose in relating the parable is, as he explicitly states, to show K. how he was deluding himself about the Court. The telling of the parable is followed by a lengthy discussion in which the priest suggests a number of interpretations which have been placed upon it, but refrains from giving a hearty endorsement to any one of them. To me, the man from the country seems to resemble K., Block, and the many petitioners at the Court which K. had attended, and his progress, or rather his retrogression, resembles that of the long-time petitioners at the Court.

The course of Block's life, as he degrades himself before the Judges and Huld, is like the life course of the man from the country as he idles and deteriorates before the doorkeeper. The priest points out that the door stands always open and that despite the final words of the doorkeeper, he is in fact unable to close it. But the petitioners—K., Block, the man from the country, and the rest of them—are inattentive to the only source of saving grace. They dissipate their strength and time on unlicensed judges and helpless advocates and lack the wisdom and the faith which would surrender them to the inextinguishable radiance whose source lies beyond the door of the Law. K. would seem to fear the message; we are told that "he wanted to put it [the parable] out of his mind" (277). The priest's parting words to K. again suggest that K. has been deluded in his view of the Court which had possessed his being: " 'The Court wants nothing from you. It receives you when you come and it dismisses you when you go.' " (278)

What are we to make of the last chapter of the book relating K.'s death? Is is murder or suicide? damnation or salvation? On the evening before K.'s thirty-first birthday, he is in his lodging, formally dressed in black and apparently expecting visitors. The thought of death has been in his mind for the past year. Even on the day of his arrest the possibility of suicide had been momentarily entertained; and when the warders had insisted on his wearing a black coat to appear before the inspector, he had said, " 'But this isn't the capital charge yet' " (14). Some time later when he was in his office awaiting the arrival of his bank's Italian client, "he was more tempted by the window, where he had recently been in the habit of spending too much time, than by his desk," (250), an implication that he was considering suicide by self-defenestration. When his two visitors arrive on the last night of his life, he goes again to the window before accompanying them down the stairs and out into the streets. As he accompanies them to the stone quarry which is to be the site of his death he notices in what perfect harmony he walks with them, in "a unity such as can hardly be formed except by lifeless matter" (281). He makes only one momentary effort of resistance, and on the whole experiences a sense of relief, deliberately fleeing from a patrolling policeman rather than soliciting his help. The whole macabre scene is none the less a peaceful one: "The moon shone down on everything with that simplicity and serenity which no other light possesses" (284). Just before the fatal knife thrust by one of his companions (he has declined to manipulate the knife himself), he envisions a human figure leaning out of a high and distant window toward him and stretching out both arms. He wonders if it may not be a friend—or indeed mankind—reaching out to help him. Asking where the invisible Judge and the impenetrable Court are, he raises his hands and spreads out all his fingers. The fatal stab accomplished, he utters his dying words " 'Like a dog!' " (286)

II

In the biblical story the first error of judgment is committed by Eve: mistaking her real judge, she lends more of an ear to the will of the serpent and to her own will than to the will of Jahweh. Adam makes the same mistake. But they soon learn that there is only one true Judge, whose will is supreme and whose verdicts stand. Summoned by God from their hiding places in the garden, Adam and Eve become the parents of the world's first alibis. Adam blames the Lord for giving him Eve and blames Eve for giving him the apple: " 'The woman whom thou gavest to be with me, she gave me fruit of the tree, and I ate' " (Genesis 3:12). Eve immediately shifts the blame to the serpent: " 'The serpent beguiled me, and I ate' " (Genesis 3:13). The serpent remains speechless! Jahweh's individual judgments on the serpent, Eve, and Adam are culminated by his decree that the man and woman must leave Eden.

Nothing is given more emphasis in the Old Testament than God's role as Judge. Great care is taken to show man precisely how he will fare if he follows the Lord's statutes and observes his commandments, and how he will fare if he does not. Chapter 26 of Leviticus and Chapter 28 of Deuteronomy are particularly enlightening in this respect. The righteous man can expect every conceivable kind of fruitfulness and prosperity: the rains will fall in season, the land will yield its increase, the trees will bear fruit, evil beasts will be held at bay, enemies will be routed, the womb will be fruitful, and the Lord will be present. But woe to those who spurn God's laws and break his covenant: the land will not yield, the trees will not bear fruit, the cattle will not increase; every form of consumption, fever, plague, pestilence, boils, ulcers, scurvy, and itch will befall the unrighteous; they will be utterly under the power of their enemies—they will be robbed of their homes, their wives, and their children; they will eat the offspring of their own bodies and will be rent by intrafamily dissension. Such judgments will be visited not only upon individuals but upon kingdoms as well; much of the Books of Kings tells of the prosperity which comes to the kingdoms of those rulers who follow God's ways, and of the desolation which falls upon the kingdoms of unrighteous monarchs. Early Israel, certainly until the questioning Job, was generally disposed to believe in an unfailing causal relationship between a man's or a community's obedience or disobedience to God and the individual's or community's measure of health or affliction.

If the Israelites emphasized God's role as Judge, they also stressed his goodness in revealing to them the Law by which they would be judged. Indeed, they viewed the gift of the Law as one of the greatest blessings which God had bestowed upon them. Jahweh had not only chosen them as his particular people; he had also given them, through revelation to Moses, a precise guide for their conduct. They knew what was expected of them and that those who, with God's grace, kept his commandments would find favor in his eyes. Thus the most cherished ambition of the Jew was to know and to follow the Law. His gratefulness to God and his prayer that he may be obedient to God's Law are best expressed in the opening verses of Psalm 119:

Blessed are those whose way is blameless,
    who walk in the law of the Lord!
Blessed are those who keep his testimonies,
    who seek him with their whole heart,
who also do no wrong,
    but walk in his ways!

Thou hast commanded thy precepts
    to be kept diligently.
O that my ways may be steadfast
    in keeping thy statutes!
Then I shall not be put to shame,
    having my eyes fixed on all thy commandments.
I will praise thee with an upright heart,
    when I learn thy righteous ordinances.
I will observe thy statutes;
    O forsake me not utterly! (1-8)

Many of the words and activities of Jesus seemed to some of his contemporaries to abrogate the Law. His attitude toward the Sabbath and toward certain dietary practices, for example, appeared rather cavalierish to the Pharisees, who were quick to rebuke him. His view of the Law, a view whose core is in the passage "the letter killeth, but the spirit giveth life" (KJV), is given most fully in the Sermon on the Mount, and his eagerness to dispel any thought that he may be setting himself against the Law is evident: "Think not that I have come to abolish the law and the prophets; I have come not to abolish them but to fulfill them. For truly, I say to you, till heaven and earth pass away, not an iota, not a dot, will pass from the law until all is accomplished." (Matthew 5:17-18)

The sanctity of the Law remains, though its followers are now promised a future blessedness rather than the material prosperities enumerated in the Pentateuch. Moreover, the gaining of the kingdom of heaven is related not only to man's walking in the commandments but also to the Person of Jesus. In the thirteenth chapter of Luke, the entrance to the kingdom is limited to a "narrow door," and the householder who determines the shutting of the door is the Lord. The Gospel of John is even more emphatic and explicit than the Synoptic Gospels in its insistence on the narrow way. The good shepherd, who is Jesus, leads his sheep through the door of the sheepfold to the kingdom of heaven, and anyone who "climbs in by another way, that man is a thief and a robber" (John 10:1). The way to blessedness is no longer described in the terms of Psalm 119, but of Jesus Christ, and when Thomas complains that he does not know the way, Jesus answers him: "I am the way, and the truth, and the life; no one comes to the Father, but by me." (John 14:6)

It was, of course, Paul, "a Hebrew born of Hebrews, as to the law a Pharisee, . . . as to righteousness under the law blameless" (Philippians 3:5-6), who effected the greatest change in the biblical view of the Law. His position is stated most succinctly in Galatians and in the seventh chapter of Romans. The Law, he insists, has served a noble purpose. Distinguishing between righteous and unrighteous action, the Law has made clear to man the nature of sin (Romans 7:7). Before the incarnation the Law served as a restraining influence; it acted as a custodian until the time of Christ, but the presence of faith makes a custodian no longer necessary (Galatians 3:23-26). That the Law is not necessary to salvation is shown by the fact that Abraham, who lived before the giving of the Law, was redeemed through his faith in God. (Galatians 3:6)

The Law, then, was a necessary preliminary to salvation, but taken by itself, it is self-defeating. For unless one keeps all the commandments he is cursed (Galatians 3:10), and it was evident to Paul, through his own nurturing under the Law and through his unstinting effort to follow its every detail, that no human being could keep its manifold commandments; consequently, every man who sought his salvation through the Law was under a curse, and he who, after the Lord's coming, continued to seek justification through it, was severed from Christ (Galatians 5:4). In short, the Christian serves "not under the old written code but in the new life of the Spirit" (Romans 7:6); "as it is written, 'He who through faith is righteous shall live'" (Romans 1:17); "a man is not justified by works of the law but through faith in Jesus Christ." (Galatians 2:16)

We have come a long way from Psalm 119 and, indeed, some way from the Sermon on the Mount. It is not that Paul denies the rightness of the commandments of the Law; he would not dispute its tenets, but he would urge that to say that the keeping of the Law is the road to righteousness, is to put the cart before the horse. Paul, and after him Luther and Calvin especially, was convinced that God gave man the gift of righteousness which in itself effected the walking in the ways of the Law. According to Paul the Pharisees of his time had dimmed their eyes to the centrality of God's grace and had placed too much confidence in a righteousness of their own, a self-righteousness. Jesus' parable of the Pharisee and the publican is most apropos.

From the Pauline point of view, then, what is the condition of the man who seeks to justify himself through the keeping of the Law? Probably the most accurate description would be to say that he endures a continual frustration. He learns in time that persistent and painstaking as he may be, he is simply unable to make of himself a righteous man acceptable to God. If he refrains from murder and adultery, he probably fails to stifle his anger or to curb a wandering and lustful eye. And if he succeeds in eradicating his irascibility and his concupiscence, he probably finds it impossible not to covet. And if, as is most unlikely, he succeeds in avoiding covetousness as well, he falls to pride, a pride in his own success. Such, for example, was even Luther's experience despite fifteen centuries of New Testament teaching behind him. When he became a monk, he sought in every way and through all kinds of rigorous asceticism —fasting, vigils, self-torture—to mortify his body to the glory of God and thus to make himself worthy of Him. But he found that his efforts led only to a self-righteous sense of personal achievement, not a sense of closer relationship to the Lord. As one becomes aware of his losing battle to work his way to God, he must indeed fall into a terrible sense of frustration, knowing that his own best efforts lead him only along the dead-end path of an ever-contracting circle. And as one becomes aware that he has guided himself into a labyrinth from which no exit can be fashioned by a human hand, he will perhaps be counseled by his self-despair to seek redemption by an other than human hand.

III

"Man that is born of a woman
    is of few days, and full of trouble.
He comes forth like a flower, and withers;
    he flees like a shadow, and continues not.

And dost thou open thy eyes upon such a one
   and bring him into judgment with thee?
Who can bring a clean thing out of an unclean?
   There is not one.
Since his days are determined,
   and the number of his months is with thee,
   and thou hast appointed his bounds that he cannot pass,
look away from him, and desist,
   that he may enjoy, like a hireling, his day."

(Job 14:1-6)

Albert Camus, early in *The Myth of Sisyphus*, states that the age of thirty is a crucial period in the life of a man. At thirty man gains a new awareness of the meaning and inexorability of time; he suddenly sees time as the enemy that it is. Camus' observation, as well as Job's lament, is relevant to *The Trial*. Joseph K.'s "arrest," as it is called, takes place on the morning of his thirtieth birthday; he dies on the evening before his thirty-first birthday.

The arrest makes best sense when interpreted allegorically. It certainly makes little sense to K. on a literal level; his country, as he tells us, enjoys a respected legal system, and he is guilty of no specific crime. When we note, however, that K. rings the bell which summons the warder, that he "in a way admitted the stranger's right to superintend his actions" (4-5), that he is not really very much surprised by his arrest even though he can recall no offense, we begin to infer that K. must have some kind of conviction of guilt, even if it is not at a fully conscious level. Furthermore, the reader is disposed to take with some seriousness the warder's contention that the legal officials "never go hunting for crime in the populace, but, as the

Law decrees, are drawn toward the guilty" (10), and one begins to feel that in some way there lies in K. a guilt which, having lain dormant, now exerts some magnetic and semiparalyzing force. If it is difficult to justify K.'s arrest on any literal level, it is easier to explain it in its relationship to a sensitive and thoughtful person of about thirty years old: K. has been brought to a conviction of sin. His sudden unrest is caused by his sudden awareness of uncleanliness, not growing out of any specific, identifiable crime, but out of his first shattering apprehension of the human condition. He marks his discovery with a celebration of a black mass by breakfasting on "a fine apple" (12)— doubtlessly with a vision of Adam pronouncing "This do in remembrance of me"!

> "Behold, I cry out, 'Violence!' but I am not answered;
>   I call aloud, but there is no justice.
>   He has walled up my way, so that I cannot pass,
>   and he has set darkness upon my paths.
>   He has stripped from me my glory,
>   and taken the crown from my head.
>   He breaks me down on every side, and I am gone,
>   and my hope has he pulled up like a tree.
>   He has kindled his wrath against me,
>   and counts me as his adversary.
>   His troops come on together;
>   they have cast up siegeworks against me,
>   and encamp round about my tent." (Job 19:7-12)

The frustration and despair voiced in this passage well reflects K.'s spirit as long as he sought to plead his case before the Court in the tenement attic of his city. Defendants are *never* acquitted by this Court, a fact that is implied by K.'s Uncle Albert and explicitly affirmed by Titorelli. Though Block has attentively studied "every precept of duty, piety, and tradition" (240), though he has struggled with the "scriptures" given to him by Huld, he has made no progress in his five years before the Court. A defendant before this Court is in a hopeless position. The best that he can do is to put off the evil day by seeking refuge in an ostensible acquittal or an indefinite postponement, both of which prevent, for the time being at least, the pronouncement of a sentence. But if they prevent a sentence, they also prevent an acquittal, leaving the accused in a terrible limbo which reduces him to the pitiful condition of a Block. It is obvious that the Court and all that it implies can never open the door to salvation. Man can struggle endlessly in his own behalf and he can solicit the services of any number of other human beings in his behalf, but no amount of such labor and striving will avail him anything.

This being so, the man who would be redeemed must look beyond himself and his fellows. When at the first interrogation K. tells the Court that "it is only a trial if I recognize it as such" (51), he speaks with some wisdom; for though every man is always on trial and under judgment, he is under no compulsion to stand before the Court to which K. is speaking. A man may choose to appear before this Court, convinced that he can establish his innocence, but since all men are guilty, he can in this way only put off the inevitable sentence of guilt. But his mistake lies in seeking to establish the impossible and to gain an acquittal from those who have not the power to acquit. It occurs to

K., before he hears the parable of the man from the country and the doorkeeper, that the priest may point to some way of breaking away from the Court altogether, the possibility of which is affirmed in the priest's final words to him: " 'The Court wants nothing from you. It receives you when you come and it dismisses you when you go.' " (278)

It would seem, then, imperative to proceed without recourse to the Court, at least to the lower Court before which K. has appeared. But the alternative is truly terrifying, calling as it does for a courageous journey into the unknown, a surrendering oneself to the judgment of a higher Court which is hinted at in legends but which has never held visible session within the space and time of the world known to K. Leni assures K. that "the higher officials keep themselves well hidden" (135); Titorelli tells him that the highest Court, which alone has "the power to grant a final acquittal . . . is quite inaccessible to you, to me, and to all of us" (197), and that word of the acquittals granted by that Court has never been officially recorded but has reached man by means of legends, "the majority of [which] are about acquittals" (193). Ironically, it is from Block, cowed and broken in spirit, that K. learns of the "great lawyers," those who are reputed to exist beyond the limits of Block's world and who bear a striking contrast to the lawyers of Block's experience:

> "There's hardly an accused man who doesn't spend some time dreaming of them after hearing about them. Don't you give way to that temptation. I have no idea who the great lawyers are and I don't believe they can be got at. I know of no single instance in which it could be defi-

nitely asserted that they had intervened. They do defend
certain cases, but one cannot achieve that oneself. They
only defend those whom they wish to defend, and they
never take action, I should think, until the case is already
beyond the province of the lower Court. In fact, it's
better to put them out of one's mind altogether, or else
one finds interviews with ordinary lawyers so stale and
stupid, with their niggling counsels and proposals—I have
experienced it myself—that one feels like throwing the
whole thing up and taking to bed with one's face to the
wall. And of course that would be stupider still, for even
in bed one wouldn't find peace." (223)

Block, without knowing it, may have the key to redemption in his own hand, but he lacks the strength to try to
push on to a Mediator in contrast with whom Huld is a
misled and misleading dwarf.

The last chapter of *The Trial* is, like much of the rest of
the novel, ambiguous. The central question is whether K.
ends in defeat, a victim of the Court which has no power of
acquittal, or ends in victory, surrendering himself willingly
to the merciful judgment of the highest Court. Has he
thrown the whole thing up, "taking to bed with [his] face to
the wall," and, finding no peace there, forcing a catastrophic
showdown with the lower Court, or does he throw himself
upon the mercy of the "great lawyers" and demand that the
"inaccessible" Court become accessible? Does he in defeat
acknowledge the strength of the doorkeeper, or does he in
victory walk past him, finding him considerably less powerful than he had claimed? In brief, is K. damned or saved?

Kafka's novel does not answer the question. One might
argue from the text that K. is damned and that the last

pages in which the two pasty visitors lead K. to his death
are a kind of re-enaction of the very end of the parable
related by the priest. K.'s complaint to the priest that the
"doorkeeper gave the message of salvation to the man only
when it could no longer help him" (269-270) might also
be applied to those moments before his own death: for
when K. was taken to the quarry and beheld the distant
figure leaning forward and stretching out his arms toward
him, it may have been too late for salvation. Perhaps we are
to understand that K. had so frittered away his capacities
elsewhere that he now lacked the time and the strength
to reach, or to be reached by, the vision and, instead, must
die "like a dog," with the terrible knowledge that he might
have been saved had he known earlier of the existence of
such a figure and placed his faith in him.

Or one might argue that K. is saved, that on the last
evening of his life he is in effect saying with Job, " 'But
I would speak to the Almighty, and I desire to argue my
case with God' " (13:3). The moon which shines down
upon him in his death quarry and possesses a "simplicity
and serenity which no other light possesses" is a hopeful
symbol. And K.'s vision of the compassionate friend who
stretches out his arms toward him and to whom he "raise[s]
his hands and spread[s] out all his fingers" (286) may be
the revelation of the Redeemer who makes himself accessible to those who seek him. It is true that the physical act
of K.'s death was, along with the acts of his life, shameful.
The knife was in his heart—" 'Like a dog!' he said; it was
as if the shame of it must outlive him" (286). But the
nature of man's death does not always possess the dignity

which he may desire, and K.'s last words might find an appropriate coda, again in Job's words:

> "For I know that my Redeemer lives,
>   and at last he will stand upon the earth;
> and after my skin has been thus destroyed,
>   then without my flesh I shall see God,
> whom I shall see on my side,
>   and my eyes shall behold, and not another.
> My heart faints within me!" (19:25-27)

But if the novel does not resolve the problem of K.'s ultimate destiny, about which we are left in doubt at the end, it does offer two definite statements about the human condition. The first is that salvation is absolutely beyond the power of man. K. makes clear on his death march that the year's trial has taught him at least one truth, namely, its utter futility: he has finally been brought to the conviction that it is futile to argue an innocence which does not exist and to look to oneself or any other human being for an acquittal which is not his to give. The other statement is that, however inaccessible it may seem, there nevertheless *is* a "radiance that streams inextinguishably from the door of the Law." We can say then that man cannot save himself and that there is a radiance of Being which has the power of salvation. But whether K. is saved or, indeed, whether the Redeemer redeems is a question left unanswered by Kafka's *The Trial*. If grace does abound, it does so only on the other side of the dark curtain of death.

4.

THE THEME OF SUFFERING:

William Faulkner's *The Sound and the Fury*

*"Behold, I have refined you, but not like silver; I have
tried you in the furnace of affliction."* (Isaiah 48:10)

I

The title of William Faulkner's novel, *The Sound and
the Fury*,* taken from Macbeth's description of life as "a
tale/ Told by an idiot, full of sound and fury,/ Signifying
nothing," is in one sense ironic. Though part of the novel
is told by an idiot and though at least one of its characters,
Mr. Compson, would probably agree that life signifies
nothing, the tale itself affirms the significance of life to
those who are willing to accept, endure, and overcome the
suffering which inevitably lies at its heart. Not only does
the novel affirm the significance of life, a characteristic
which it shares in common with innumerable writings of
less vision and more piety and sentimentality; the novel is
of highest significance itself, taking its place in this respect
with the novels of Hawthorne and Melville and certainly

---

* In this chapter, all excerpts from *The Sound and the Fury* by
William Faulkner are used by the permission of the publisher, Random House, Inc., New York. Page references are to the Modern
Library edition, 1946.

110

being of equal significance with any American novel since the time of Hawthorne and Melville. The word "significance" may, of course, be construed in many ways; by it I mean that quality which perceives the human condition in its greatest complexity and presents it with absolute integrity and consistency. *The Sound and the Fury* is an excursion into human souls, a journey unfolding the depths and variations of depravity without surrendering to the despair which most of the journey would seem to evoke, but does not evoke because of the constant reminder that there are always those who, like Dilsey, endure and win the crown which comes to persons willing to accept with equanimity all the deprivations which life can and does inflict.

The novel is difficult, and the difficulty is necessary, which is to say that the very greatness of the book depends in large part upon the complexity of its form. In addition to an introductory appendix sketching the Compson family tree, there are four parts. The first three are in the stream of consciousness style and are narrated by Benjy Compson, Quentin Compson, and Jason Compson on April 7, 1928, June 2, 1910, and April 6, 1928, respectively. The last part is narrated in the third person, has the servant Dilsey at its center, and takes place on Easter Sunday, April 8, 1928. The difficulty lies in the first two parts, as they present to us the impressions of the idiot Benjy on his thirty-third birthday and of Quentin on the day of his suicide. In both sections there are many time changes as a present event recalls a past one in the consciousness of the narrator; the time changes are indicated in the text by the transition from normal print to italics or vice versa. Since the stream of consciousness style is bare of the many clarifying transitions from impression to impression or thought to thought which a third-person narrator would feel called upon to make, and since Benjy's idiot mind and Quentin's exceedingly complex mind are both somewhat distant from that of the average reader, the problem of following the text is a considerable one. But a second reading of the novel (the first reading is not enough) will, I think, persuade the reader that Faulkner has chosen the method of presentation which reveals most deeply and most precisely the nature and dilemma of the book's characters. Faulkner is not simply ingenious; he has made the near-perfect marriage of form and content in which the style is most adequate in presenting the matter which he wishes to unfold. The reader's gradual success in seeing how the many parts of the narrative are interrelated is a tremendously exciting experience, as he notes how a superb craftsman and a profound observer has gone about the task of writing a major work in the history of the novel.

One of the novel's central themes, that of suffering, will be the concern of this chapter. The Compson family had more than their share of it, and the novel is in great part the story of how they reacted to its presence. If one can view the Compson's servant Dilsey as Faulkner's representative of a human soul "capable of compassion and sacrifice and endurance," then Dilsey's reaction to the suffering which is her lot is the reaction of man at his best; she faces with full responsibility the burden which falls upon her. And if this is so, then each member of the Compson family (with the rather ambiguous exception of Benjy) fails to accept his own burden with a fully human responsibility, and each fails in his own way.

Mr. Compson seeks to put himself beyond the reach of suffering through a philosophy of negation and a decanter of whisky. He shields himself from disappointment by reducing his expectations of man to zero. No battle is ever won or even fought, he tells Quentin; "the field only reveals to man his own folly and despair, and victory is an illusion of philosophers and fools" (95). A man "is the sum of his misfortunes" (123); he is a "problem in impure properties carried tediously to an unvarying nil: stalemate of dust and desire" (142-143). Man has neither reason for being nor purpose in living; he is "conceived by accident," has the dice constantly loaded against him, and must come to realize that not even his "despair or remorse or bereavement is . . . particularly important to the dark diceman," that aloof god who cares nothing for the creation (196). Man is not a creature of blood and is not saved by the blood of anyone else: ". . . all men are just accumulations dolls stuffed with sawdust swept up from the trash heaps where all previous dolls had been thrown away the sawdust flowing from what wound in what side that not for me died not" (194). People are so inconsequential that they are not even capable of committing an enormity: ". . . they cannot do anything very dreadful at all they cannot even remember tomorrow what seemed dreadful today" (99). Such a philosophy is, of course, an evasion of all responsibilities; suffering is unaccepted and unacceptable and is veiled in the golden-brown haze of alcoholic oblivion.

The novel's most odious character, Mrs. Compson, evades

her responsibilities through a nauseating self-pity and a convenient hypochondria. Mr. Compson, despite his philosophy, was at least possessed by a certain tenderness; in Mrs. Compson it is difficult to discover any appealing characteristic, unless perhaps it be her regard for Jason. The sum of her feeling for Benjy is neatly summed up in his presence: " 'It's a judgment on me' " (25). When she learns of her daughter Caddy's sexual irregularities, she can respond to them only as they affect her own feelings: ". . . I thought that Benjamin was punishment enough for any sins I have committed I thought he was my punishment for putting aside my pride and marrying a man who held himself above me . . ." (122). And her reaction to Quentin's suicide shows again her incredibly exclusive concern for herself: " 'What reason did Quentin have? Under God's heaven what reason did he have? It can't be simply to flout and hurt me. Whoever God is, He would not permit that. I'm a lady. You might not believe that from my offspring, but I am' " (315). This brief sampling of Mrs. Compson's remarks and the manner in which she shut herself off in her room, demanding that others cater to her hypochondriacal peculiarities, are enough to show her total irresponsibility to the suffering world about her.

The relationship of Benjy to the theme of suffering is considerably less obvious than that of the other Compsons. That he suffered is clear enough, but it is doubtful that an idiot can be said to meet suffering or to deal with it in any responsible way. His greatest suffering resulted from the deprivation of two of the three things which he loved— Caddy, first of all, whose home was forbidden to her after her tragic affair with Dalton Ames and her tragic marriage with Sydney Herbert Head; and second, the Compson pasture, sold to pay for Caddy's wedding and Quentin's freshman year at Harvard, and converted into a golf course. Benjy is forever at the fence separating the reduced Compson property from the golf course and forever moaning as the cries of "caddie" remind him of the loss of his sister. Presumed to be deaf and dumb, he nevertheless responds to sounds, and his uncanny intuitiveness brings upon him frequent and considerable pain and occasional pleasure. He cries at any time mention is made of Caddy's leaving and is soothed by her assurance that she will not go. To his sense of smell there are innumerable references; he is never happier than when Caddy "smells like trees," and he is desolate when she uses perfume. He can smell death and sickness, as we learn both from his own stream of consciousness and from Dilsey's husband, Roskus, who speaks of Benjy's intuitiveness and his unfailing instinct for approaching death: " 'He know lot more than folks thinks. He knowed they time was coming, like that pointer done. He could tell you when hisn coming, if he could talk. Or yours. Or mine.' " (51). And he can tell from Caddy's very presence and from her eyes when she was first seduced. Quentin, thinking back to Caddy's surrender to Dalton Ames, affirms that Benjy "took one look at her and knew" (119), a fact made clear in other parts of the novel (87, 168). At the mercy of his delicate senses, he suffers. Castrated at the instigation of Jason in 1913, constantly terrorized by the slightest deviation from the normal order of his pathetic life, he is finally committed after his mother's death in 1933 to the State Asylum by Jason. The whole pattern of his life is one of suffering, though to measure and pass judgment on his response to his burden is perhaps impossible.

If Mr. Compson fortified himself against his day-to-day world through philosophical nihilism and alcohol, and Mrs. Compson did so through self-pity and hypochondria, then their son Quentin frustrated the suffering which was his through suicide. Quentin was possessed by a concept of family honor which to him was to be judged solely in terms of Caddy's virginity or loss of it; it was an honor "precariously and (he knew well) only temporarily supported by the minute fragile membrane of her maidenhead just as a miniature replica of all the whole vast globy earth may be poised on the nose of a trained seal" (9). So zealously would he have guarded this honor and so fondly did he love Caddy that he would have preferred an incestuous relationship with her to her seduction by one outside the family, Dalton Ames. Unlike his father, he felt that man did have the freedom and power to commit an enormity, and he desperately wished to believe that the sin of incest would be the means whereby he could lead his sister and himself into hell, where they could eternally live together keeping the Compson honor intact and enshrined. Their sin would be so dreadful that all the other occupants of hell would flee from them in horror: *"Then you will have only me then only me then the two of us amid the pointing and the horror beyond the clean flame"* (135). Then they could be beyond the sound and the fury of this pain-giving world. To his father Quentin even insisted that he—not Dalton Ames and not anyone else—was the fountain of Caddy's pregnancy. But when Caddy's maidenhead was violated, when Mr. Compson was impressed neither by Quentin's confession of incest nor by the concept of virginity, when Quentin could not in fact bring himself to commit incest or to carry through his suicide pact with Caddy (the imagery of the unsuccessful attempt at double suicide narrated on pages 168-172 is suggestive of incest, with the knife being an unmistakable phallic symbol), when all these failures convinced Quentin that the Compson honor was forever lost and that he and Caddy could never accomplish the desired lonely exile in hell, then he turned, on June 2, 1910, to his suicide in the Charles River. It was the only way left to him of escaping the unendurable pain of this world; it was his final evasion of responsibility.

Jason, "the first sane Compson since before Culloden" (16), found his bulwark against suffering in his sanity. His sanity was of a stoical nature, one which held no room for the tender sensibilities and no respect for their presence in others. He was almost as incapable as Benjy of conceptual thought and was consequently poles apart from Quentin in this respect. He shared with his mother the characteristic of judging everything in terms solely of its effect on self. Caddy's fornication was abhorrent to him not because he held a concept of Compson honor, but because its consequences finally deprived him of the promised position at her husband's bank in Indiana. He hated Caddy's bastard daughter Quentin because she served as a memory incarnate of his lost business opportunity, and he sought to block her promiscuous behavior because of its reflection on his reputation. Benjy was viewed not as a brother but as a care, as another mouth to be fed, and while he sleeps Jason refers to him with his customary wit as "the Great American Gelding snoring away like a planing mill" (280). His reaction to his brother's suicide is that of a sane and witty, though an unfeeling, man: ". . . at Harvard they teach you how to go for a swim at night without knowing how to swim" (213). His relationship with his mistress Lorraine was almost as businesslike as that with his boss Earl; in both cases a contract was to be strictly observed and carried out to the untender letter of the law. A creature of Jason's uncompromising independence—twice he boasts "I can stand on my own feet" (224, 229)—is unlikely to suffer from any sense of compassion for or responsibility to other people. Life becomes a matter of pitting one's own strength or cleverness against that of other people, and pain comes only upon being outmaneuvered or outwitted. Miss Quentin's great material victory over Jason drives him to rage, but neither to insanity nor to suicide; it catches him in the stomach but not in the heart. He survives it and lives out his life in sanity, the kind of sanity that protects him from the terrible psychical or spiritual torment that may fall upon the compassionate.

Dilsey alone can stand up to the sound and the fury of life with courage, tenderness, and endurance; of her and her kind Faulkner writes in the prefatory appendix to the novel the simple and accurate statement: "They endured" (22). One fruitful approach to Dilsey's character is to place it constantly in juxtaposition with that of Mrs. Compson, for we find that Dilsey is to the Compson family everything that Mrs. Compson should be. Dilsey is in fact the mother of the family; when Miss Quentin is brought in her inglorious infancy to the Compson home, Dilsey says with truth: " 'I raised all of them and I reckon I can raise one more' " (51). While Mrs. Compson can view Benjy simply as a judgment upon her, it is Dilsey who affords him real love; typical of her care of him is this passage toward the end of the book: "Dilsey led Ben to the bed and drew him down beside her and she held him, rocking back and forth, wiping his drooling mouth upon the hem of her skirt. 'Hush, now,' she said, stroking his head, 'Hush. Dilsey got you' " (332). And if she serves as nurse to Benjy, she serves as constant protector of the unwanted Miss Quentin. That Mrs. Compson was no mother is evident not only to the reader, but to Caddy and Quentin as well; on the day of his suicide he recalls Caddy's earlier words, *"if I'd just had a mother so I could say Mother Mother"* (190). Of supreme irony is Mrs. Compson's remark about Miss Quentin, spoken in the light of Caddy's sexual indiscretions: " 'If she could grow up never to know that she had a mother, I would thank God' " (217).

Ironic also is Mrs. Compson's constant affirmation that she has sacrificed for and suffered for her family. To Jason she says, " '. . . it's my place to suffer for my children' " (238), and " 'I was raised to believe that people would deny themselves for their own flesh and blood' " (279). Of Caddy, who knows that she has never had a mother. Mrs. Compson says in her self-pitying manner: "I've suffered for her dreamed and planned and sacrificed I went down into the valley" (121). It is Dilsey, of course, who quietly fulfills the role of sacrificer and sufferer which Mrs. Compson claims for herself, and it is to Dilsey that Mrs. Compson addresses these words of fine dramatic irony: " 'You're not the one who has to bear it. It's not your responsibility. You can go away. You dont have to bear the brunt of it day in and day out.' " (288)

It takes only an account of one day in Dilsey's life to show who is the true center of sacrifice and suffering in *The Sound and the Fury*. As she painfully and faithfully hobbles through her chores on Easter day of 1928, we sense the real meaning of endurance. The physical description of Dilsey on that morning is suggestive of her character:

> She had been a big woman once but now her skeleton rose, draped loosely in unpadded skin that tightened again upon a paunch almost dropsical, as though muscle and tissue had been courage or fortitude which the days or the years had consumed until only the indomitable skeleton was left rising like a ruin or a landmark above the somnolent and impervious guts, and above that the collapsed face that gave the impression of the bones themselves being outside the flesh, lifted into the driving day with an expression at once fatalistic and of a child's astonished disappointment, until she turned and entered the house again and closed the door. (282)

The skeleton and guts are enough to see the Compsons through another day, and as Mrs. Compson nags at her Negro servant from the vantage point of her hypochondria, Dilsey carries logs from woodpile to kitchen, starts the fire, tends to Mrs. Compson's hot water bottle, prepares breakfast, oversees her son Luster, and still finds time to lead Benjy and her family to church. It is her presence and that alone which has prevented the Compsons from sinking into an even more complete state of collapse than has already befallen them. It is fitting so far as Dilsey is concerned that the novel ends on Easter Sunday, for it is the recollection of that day, so firmly engraved in her mind and heart by the powerful sermon of the preacher from St. Louis, which sustains her. If, on her return to the Compson home, Dilsey sees "the square, paintless house with its rotting portico" (313), a fitting symbol for the rotting lives of those within its walls, she also sees " 'de first en de last,' " " 'de beginnin, en . . . de endin' " (313), the resurrected Lord who hovers about her and has taken possession of her soul.

II

The biblical interest in the problem of suffering begins with Jahweh's judgment on Adam and Eve. Because of her sin Eve must endure the pain of childbirth and the domination of her husband; because of his sin Adam must earn his bread through the toil of his body and the sweat of his brow. It is important to note, particularly in the light of later biblical reflections on suffering, that the Mosaic account in the third chapter of Genesis is interested primarily in the *cause* of suffering: suffering is the consequence of sin. And as we saw in the preceding chapter of this book, the Pentateuch, as it turns itself frequently to the facts of misfortune and disaster in the world, does so with the constant reminder that sin is punished and virtue rewarded in this world. If a man sins he can anticipate suffering; if he is seen to suffer it can be assumed that he has sinned. Jahweh exalts the righteous and casts down the unrighteous in material and visible fashion. The twenty-sixth chapter of Leviticus and the twenty-eighth chapter of Deuteronomy contain lengthy catalogues of those blessings which will come to the obedient and of the punishments which will befall the disobedient. And the Books of Kings, with their accounts of the many kings of Israel and Judah, pursue an almost mechanical insistence that the kingdoms of those who leave the ways of Jahweh are caught in the vise of suffering, while the kingdoms of the faithful enjoy prosperity.

The most compelling biblical challenge to this view of an unfailing causal relationship between sin and suffering is found, of course, in the Book of Job, whose writer sees that the facts of one's daily life simply do not bear out the assumption of such a relationship. The narrative opens as Satan, whose main function seems to be to roam around the world and take delight in all evidences of wrongdoing, visits the Lord, who somewhat proudly asks him: " 'Have you considered my servant Job, that there is none like him on the earth, a blameless and upright man, who fears God and turns away from evil?' " Satan shows his Mosaic orthodoxy when he asks, " 'Does Job fear God for naught?' " and suggests that a man of Job's many blessings can afford to be righteous. The Lord gives Satan permission to bring upon Job any afflictions short of death, confident that Job's faith in Him will remain in spite of his suffering. Satan works with dispatch and thoroughness: Job loses his oxen, asses, sheep, camels, servants, sons, and daughters. When these calamities fail to break his spirit or destroy his faith, Satan afflicts him "with loathsome sores from the sole of his foot to the crown of his head" (2:7). Still Job continues in his faith, despite his wife's demand that he curse God. In his self-appointed comforters—Eliphaz, Bildad, and Zophar—Job is assailed with perhaps the greatest of his afflictions. His well-meaning friends, firm in their conviction that the presence of suffering is proof of antecedent wickedness, seek to convince Job that he need only accept that conviction and turn to righteousness if he would regain his bliss. Job's contribution to the doctrine of suffering is his refusal to accept so neat and pat an answer to the world's misery. His discourse with his friends, which begins on a calm enough note, gradually arouses tempers as their essential and crucial disagreement becomes clear. The confidence which the "comforters" have in the causal relationship between sin and suffering is seen perhaps most acutely when Eliphaz inaccurately accuses Job of the most outlandish behavior, of deeds which Job never committed but which he is assumed, on the basis of his grievous suffering, to have committed:

"Is not your wickedness great?
     There is no end to your iniquities.
For you have exacted pledges of your brothers for
          nothing,
     and stripped the naked of their clothing.
You have given ño water to the weary to drink,
     and you have withheld bread from the hungry.
The man with power possessed the land,
     and the favored man dwelt in it.
You have sent widows away empty,
     and the arms of the fatherless were crushed.

Therefore snares are round about you,
    and sudden terror overwhelms you;
your light is darkened, so that you cannot see,
    and a flood of waters covers you." (22:5-11)

Job, knowing the falsity of the charge, desires above all to take his case to the Lord; as he says somewhat earlier: " 'But I would speak to the Almighty,/ and I desire to argue my case with God' " (13:3).

Jahweh's answer to Job, though perhaps inconclusive so far as the problem of suffering is concerned, is nevertheless a refutation of the view held by Eliphaz and his comrades. The Lord, with some sarcasm, convinces Job of his own omnipotence and omniscience and of Job's frailty and ignorance, asserting that it is not man's place to contend with the Almighty or to question his ways; man is to accept his condition, whatever it is, and have faith in the Lord. Job's victory is twofold: he has already renounced the false doctrine of his companions, and he now capitulates completely to the Lord's power and wisdom:

"I had heard of thee by the hearing of the ear,
    but now my eye sees thee;
therefore I despise myself,
    and repent in dust and ashes." (42:5-6)

The Lord rebukes Eliphaz, Bildad, and Zophar for their false doctrine; praises Job for his refusal to succumb to it; tells the three companions that Job's prayer for them will protect them from being treated as they deserve; and bestows upon Job twice as much as he had before his trial. If these final gifts would seem in a sense to destroy the very argument which the Book of Job seeks to present, it should be remembered that the writer of Job held no belief in a life beyond death, a life which promised peace to those who had met the trials of this life with faith and endurance.

Of most importance in the biblical concept of suffering is the development from a concern with the *cause* of suffering to a concern with its *purpose* and *effect*. The Pentateuch, the Books of Kings, the companions of Job, all seek primarily to account for its cause. The Book of Job is a rather devastating challenge to the earlier tradition, though the answer which it gives to the problem is not totally satisfactory; in some ways it seems more an acquittal of God than of man. But in both the Old Testament and the New there are many affirmations of the positive value of suffering for man. Interest lies not so much in its cause as in its effect, and it comes to be looked upon not so much as a curse but as a blessing. The writer of Psalm 119 sees in affliction a noble purpose, that of leading a man to follow God's Law: "Before I was afflicted I went astray;/ but now I keep thy word" (67), and "It is good for me that I was afflicted,/ that I might learn thy statutes" (71). Proverbs asserts that suffering is a special mark of God's favor, to be visited upon his sons: "My son, do not despise the Lord's discipline/ or be weary of his reproof, /for the Lord reproves him whom he loves,/ as a father the son in whom he delights" (3:11-12).

Virtually the whole of the New Testament is a glorification of suffering. When Peter, hearing Jesus' statement that he must suffer and be killed, responds with a " 'God forbid, Lord!' " Jesus rebukes him: " 'Get behind me, Satan!

You are a hindrance to me; for you are not on the side of God, but of men' " (Matthew 16:21-23). And Jesus goes on to point out that the self-denial and suffering which are involved in following the way of the Cross are the very means to salvation:

> "If any man would come after me, let him deny himself and take up his cross and follow me. For whoever would save his life will lose it, and whoever loses his life for my sake will find it. For what will it profit a man, if he gains the whole world and forfeits his life? Or what shall a man give in return for his life? For the Son of man is to come with his angels in the glory of his Father, and then he will repay every man for what he has done." (Matthew 16:24-27)

Various epistles and other writings of the New Testament carry on the same tradition. To the Romans Paul emphasizes enthusiastically the wonderful purpose and effect of suffering; he writes of the joy of suffering, "knowing that suffering produces endurance, and endurance produces character, and character produces hope, and hope does not disappoint us, because God's love has been poured into our hearts through the Holy Spirit which has been given to us" (5:3-5), and he insists that "the sufferings of this present time are not worth comparing with the glory that is to be revealed to us" (8:18). The writer of Hebrews urges his readers to look to Jesus, "who for the joy that was set before him endured the cross, despising the shame, and is seated at the right hand of the throne of God" (12:2), and he writes that though discipline seems painful while one endures it, yet, "later it yields the peaceful fruit of righteousness to those who have been trained by it" (12:11). James writes in the same vein, saying that trial is a blessing, leading as it does to the crown of life for the faithfully enduring one (1:12). And the principal exhortation of the apocalyptic Revelation to John is that the persecuted Christians remain firm in their faith that they may finally be accepted into the kingdom of God.

We have seen that in earlier biblical thought suffering was viewed primarily in terms of its cause, but that in much Old Testament thought and in most of the New Testament writings, suffering becomes a mark of the Lord's favor, a tender discipline upon his chosen ones; the way of the Cross, a way of self-denial and persecution, is the way to salvation. There is still another biblical view of affliction and a very important one; it is of an affliction willingly endured, and springing not so much from a view of future glory as from one's love for another. It lies at the heart of Jesus' great commandment to his disciples in the Fourth Gospel: " 'This is my commandment, that you love one another as I have loved you. Greater love has no man than this, that a man lay down his life for his friends' " (15:12-13). And when a man is willing not only to lay down his life for his friends, but also to lay down his life in atonement for the sins of his friends, then we reach the very core of Christian doctrine. This is the doctrine of vicarious suffering—suffering for others—and it is seen in the Cross of Jesus Christ; it is the means whereby God reconciles sinful man to Himself through Christ. In Christ "all the fullness of God was pleased to dwell, and through him to reconcile to himself all things, whether on earth or in heaven, making peace by the blood of his cross. And you, who once were estranged and hostile in mind, doing evil deeds, he has now reconciled in his body of flesh by his death, in order to present you holy and blameless and irreproachable before him, provided that you continue in the faith. . ." (Colossians 1:19-23).

Perhaps the most famous biblical passage on vicarious suffering is found in the Old Testament, in Second Isaiah. It is known as the Suffering Servant passage, and it has been viewed by some Christian commentators as a foreshadowing of and a pattern of the life of Christ. It is so central to any discussion of the biblical concept of suffering and so relevant to *The Sound and the Fury* that full quotation is justified:

Behold, my servant shall prosper,
    he shall be exalted and lifted up,
    and shall be very high.
As many were astonished at him—
    his appearance was so marred, beyond human
        semblance,
    and his form beyond that of the sons of men—
so shall he startle many nations;
    kings shall shut their mouths because of him;
for that which has not been told them they shall see,
    and that which they have not heard they shall
        understand.
Who has believed what we have heard?
    And to whom has the arm of the Lord been revealed?
For he grew up before him like a young plant,
    and like a root out of dry ground;

he had no form or comeliness that we should look at him,
    and no beauty that we should desire him.
He was despised and rejected by men;
    a man of sorrows, and acquainted with grief;
and as one from whom men hide their faces
    he was despised, and we esteemed him not.
Surely he has borne our griefs
    and carried our sorrows;
yet we esteemed him stricken,
    smitten by God, and afflicted.
But he was wounded for our transgressions,
    he was bruised for our iniquities;
upon him was the chastisement that made us whole,
    and with his stripes we are healed.
All we like sheep have gone astray;
    we have turned every one to his own way;
and the Lord has laid on him
    the iniquity of us all.
He was oppressed, and he was afflicted,
    yet he opened not his mouth;
like a lamb that is led to the slaughter,
    and like a sheep that before its shearers is dumb,
    so he opened not his mouth.
By oppression and judgment he was taken away;
    and as for his generation, who considered
that he was cut off out of the land of the living,
    stricken for the transgression of my people?
And they made his grave with the wicked
    and with a rich man in his death,
although he had done no violence,
    and there was no deceit in his mouth.
Yet it was the will of the Lord to bruise him;
    he has put him to grief;
when he makes himself an offering for sin,
    he shall see his offspring, he shall prolong his days;

the will of the Lord shall prosper in his hand;
> he shall see the fruit of the travail of his soul and be
> satisfied;
by his knowledge shall the righteous one, my servant,
> make many to be accounted righteous;
> and he shall bear their iniquities.
Therefore I will divide him a portion with the great,
> and he shall divide the spoil with the strong;
because he poured out his soul to death,
> and was numbered with the transgressors;
yet he bore the sin of many,
> and made intercession for the transgressors.

(Isaiah 52:13—53:12)

III

Any treatment of the concept of suffering in *The Sound and the Fury* must concentrate primarily on Benjy and Dilsey, both of whom are brought to mind by the Suffering Servant passage. Mr. Compson's most philosophical contribution to the problem comes in his words to Quentin: ". . . a man is the sum of his misfortunes. One day you'd think misfortune would get tired. . ." (123). When Quentin becomes convinced of the indefatigability of misfortune, he jumps into the Charles River, weighted down with two six-pound flatirons. Mrs. Compson's whining conviction that she is misfortune's special prey leads her no farther than self-pity. Jason is interested only in material fortune or misfortune and bends all his strength toward making his own fortune with a brutal assault on any obstacles which may come in his way. But what about Benjy and Dilsey?

The greatest enigma in the novel, so far as the problem of suffering is concerned, lies in Benjy. How are we to view him? One is tempted to consider the possibility of his being a Christ figure. Most of the novel's action takes place over an Easter weekend, the Saturday of which is Benjy's thirty-third birthday. Mrs. Compson's expressed dread of Christmas (28) might be suggestive of her dread of Benjy if he is a Christ figure; and, if he is, her remark that "It's a judgment on me" (25) may be, among other things, a striking bit of dramatic irony. If the Suffering Servant passage is in part suggestive of the life of Christ, it is also in part suggestive of Benjy's life. Benjy, like Isaiah's figure, is disfigured and despised, and is a man of sorrows. The reader, who is given no physical description of Benjy until the last section of the book, is shocked by the repulsive delineation of the idiot whom he has come to view with compassion; Benjy is described as

> a big man who appeared to have been shaped of some substance whose particles would not or did not cohere to one another or to the frame which supported it. His skin was dead looking and hairless; dropsical too, he moved with a shambling gait like a trained bear. His hair was pale and fine. It had been brushed smoothly down upon his brow like that of children in daguerreotypes. His eyes were clear, of the pale sweet blue of cornflowers, his thick mouth hung open, drooling a little. (290)

That he was despised by Jason, by the occasional wooers of Caddy and Miss Quentin, and probably by Mrs. Compson, is evident; as is the fact that he was a creature of sorrows, constantly grieving at his loss of Caddy and the Compson pasture. But it is difficult to go beyond this and view in

Benjy the vicarious sufferer, an afflicted one by whose stripes others are healed, an intercessor for the transgressions of others. This is not to say, however, that he does not enjoy God's favor, and Dilsey speaks with her usual uncanny accuracy when she says of him, " '. . . de good Lawd dont keer whether he smart er not,' " (306), and says to him, " 'You's de Lawd's chile, anyway' " (333).

But it is surely Dilsey who of the novel's characters comes closest to being a Christ figure or a Suffering Servant figure. A person of no form or comeliness or beauty, one whose whole race has been despised and rejected, she is beyond this not only one who is grieved but also one who has borne the griefs of others. There could be no more apt description of the Dilseys of the world than that "They endured." Dilsey endures virtually the entire burden of the Compson family. One of the principal distinctions between Benjy's suffering and Dilsey's is that hers requires some measure of assent. All the Compsons, again excepting Benjy, evaded the responsibility which was rightfully theirs in a world in which a person might well think, with Mr. Compson, that misfortune would get tired. Benjy because of his very nature has the power of neither assent nor dissent; and if Isaiah's servant is a like powerless figure (the Isaiah passage taken simply in itself might suggest such a figure, though its context would seem to call for a conscious and willing sufferer), certainly Christ is not. Jesus in Gethsemane has a full awareness of the world's misery and of his role in relation to it: " 'Father, if thou art willing, remove this cup from me; nevertheless not my will, but thine, be done' " (Luke 22:42). To Dilsey it is the Lord's will that she endure, and her very presence in the Compson family stands as a constant judgment upon those who refuse to endure. When Jason threatens Miss Quentin with a belt, Dilsey's response is representative of her entire relationship to the Compsons: " 'Hit me, den, ef nothin else but hittin somebody wont do you. Hit me' " (203). Dilsey is mother and protectress to all the Compson children, and she is forever picking up the responsibilities which others drop.

It is Dilsey who is most at home over an Easter weekend. It is she who takes Benjy to church in memory and glorification of the resurrection of Christ, and she does so in the face of mounting criticism of those who " 'thinks he aint good enough fer white church, but nigger church aint good enough fer him' " (306). If the resurrection is an annual inconvenience to Mrs. Compson and Jason (for Dilsey's Easter churchgoing interferes with Sunday dinner), it is the very stay of Dilsey's life. The words of the preacher from St. Louis sustain the large spirit in her fatigued and debilitated body: " 'I sees de resurrection en de light; sees de meek Jesus saying Dey kilt Me dat ye shall live again; I died dat dem whut sees en believes shall never die. Breddren, O breddren! I sees de doom crack en hears de golden horns shoutin down de glory, en de arisen dead whut got de blood and de ricklickshun of de Lamb!' " (312-313)

That the transgressions and iniquities of the Compsons are borne by Dilsey is beyond doubt. She suffers because of the Compsons, and she suffers for the Compsons in the sense that she willingly bears upon her own shoulders the burdens which are properly theirs. This leaves the question of whether she is in the full sense a vicarious sufferer; that is to say, are her sufferings of benefit to the Compsons in an ultimate sense? Their lot on this earth would be more miserable without Dilsey, since they receive great benefit from her presence, but are we to conclude also that her chastisement made them whole, that her stripes healed them, that she "made intercession for the transgressors" in the same way that the Suffering Servant or Christ is affirmed to do? That she herself is to be saved is made clear; in one of the novel's flashbacks Dilsey, objecting to Mrs. Compson's changing the name of her youngest son from Maury to Benjamin, tells the young Caddy that her name will be Dilsey long after she is forgotten by the Compsons:

> *How will they know it's Dilsey, when it's long forgot, Dilsey, Caddy said.*
> *It'll be in the Book, honey, Dilsey said. Writ out.*
> *Can you read it, Caddy said.*
> *Wont have to, Dilsey said. They'll read it for me.*
> *All I got to do is say Ise here.* (77)

But the question remains whether, by means of Dilsey's selfless suffering, the names of the Compsons will be inscribed in the same book. The novel would seem to affirm that Benjy's name will appear, and perhaps those of Mr. Compson, Caddy, and Quentin, all of whom have some tenderness in their hearts in spite of their transgressions. But a reader would have to look long for any redemptive qualities in Mrs. Compson, Jason, or Miss Quentin. Fortunately, readers are spared the terrible responsibility of making any ultimate judgment. There is no doubt, however, that the figure of Dilsey may serve as the incarnate embodiment of Faulkner's faith in man, eloquently expressed in his Nobel prize speech of 1950:

> . . . I believe that man will not merely endure: he will prevail. He is immortal, not because he alone among creatures has an inexhaustible voice, but because he has a soul, a spirit capable of compassion and sacrifice and endurance.

5.

THE THEME OF LOVE:

Graham Greene's *The Heart of the Matter*

"O villain! Thou wilt be condemned into everlasting redemption for this." (Dogberry in *Much Ado About Nothing*)

I

"Why . . . do I love this place so much? Is it because here human nature hasn't had time to disguise itself? Nobody here could ever talk about a heaven on earth. Heaven remained rigidly in its proper place on the other side of death, and on this side flourished the injustices, the cruelties, the meannesses, that everywhere people so cleverly hushed up. Here you could love human beings nearly as God loved them, knowing the worst. . . ." (32)*

Perhaps it is Scobie's attempt "to love human beings nearly as God [loves] them" which leads him finally to his suicide in Graham Greene's *The Heart of the Matter*. The action of the novel takes place during World War II in a British-governed town in West Africa where Major Henry Scobie is second in command on the Colonial police force.

---

* In this chapter, all excerpts from *The Heart of the Matter* by Graham Greene are used by the permission of the publisher, The Viking Press, Inc., New York. Page references are to the Viking Press edition, 1948.

His immense compassion and his overwhelming sense of responsibility for other persons lead him to take actions in
their behalf which draw him farther and farther away
from a life which could be conceived in any orthodox way
as a virtuous or righteous one. The novel ends with the
question of whether a man who has been derelict in his
professional duties, has committed adultery, has partaken
of the Eucharist with mortal and unabsolved sin on his
soul, has acknowledged his lack of trust in God, and has
committed suicide—all presumably out of love for his
fellow men, whether this man is nevertheless the object of
God's salvation. A closely related question is whether a
man's love for man can be in conflict with his love for God:
is Scobie accurate in his reflection toward the end of the
book that human love "had robbed him of love for eternity"
(288)?

As the introductory quotation shows, Scobie is bound to
his post by its very misery, for it is in just such a place
that a love like God's is most needed. And after fifteen years
of this misery, Scobie would choose it again if he were to
begin anew. He is forever haunted by his sense of responsibility. On one occasion, as he stands looking at the lights
of a hospital housing some survivors of a shipwrecked and
terrible ordeal at sea, his heart feels the weight of all the
attendant suffering. Wondering sadly if he alone feels a
responsibility for the pain and the grief, he yet finds some
solace in his memory of Abraham's attempted intercession
for the inhabitants of Sodom (Genesis 18:23-33), and he
reflects that "in the Cities of the Plain a single soul might
have changed the mind of God." (126)

Scobie's sense of responsibility is directed toward the unattractive, who possess a strange and an infallible attraction for him:

> He had no sense of responsibility towards the beautiful and the graceful and the intelligent. They could find their own way. It was the face for which nobody would go out of his way, the face that would never catch the covert look, the face which would soon be used to rebuffs and indifference, that demanded his allegiance. (172)

His wife Louise reminds him "of a dog or a cat" (15) or, sitting on her bed under a mosquito net, of "a joint under a meat cover" (17); her face has "the yellow-ivory tinge of atabrine," and her hair is "dark and stringy with sweat" (16). And yet "these were the times of ugliness when he loved her, when pity and responsibility reached the intensity of a passion" (16). And it is the pitiableness and the ugliness of Helen Rolt, one of the survivors of the shipwreck, which exert the irresistible attraction leading to adultery. Her ugliness "was like handcuffs on his wrists" (172), and as he views her sleeping after their first amour, her position reminds him of the "odd cramped attitude of someone who has been shot in escaping," and of "a bundle of cannon fodder" (174). When Scobie sees a rested and more attractive Helen at a later time attending a party, he wonders if he would ever have fallen in love with her had she appeared so at their first meeting (209).

Scobie's attraction for the unattractive and his terrible sense of responsibility for them lead him into a life which knows little but misery and one which he views as a vale of tears. His own experience convinces him that understanding between human beings is impossible (84), that the expectation of happiness in this world is absurd (128), and that "to be a human being one [has] to drink the cup" (129). His dreams of peace and happiness, springing from his conviction that any human intimacy is fraught with pain, are always those in which he is removed from his bondage to persons for whom he feels the greatest responsibility. Could he have lived his life over again, he would have chosen the same unrewarding work and the same miserable town, but "he would not have expected any other persons to share it with him, the rat upon the bath, the lizard on the wall, the tornado blowing open the windows at one in the morning, and the last pink light upon the laterite roads at sundown" (60). Another dream in which Scobie finds perfect happiness is one in which he experiences the peace of the natural world and a freedom from any human entanglements:

> He was walking through a wide cool meadow with Ali [his loved servant] at his heels: there was nobody else anywhere in his dream, and Ali never spoke. Birds went by far overhead, and once when he sat down the grass was parted by a small green snake which passed onto his hand and up his arm without fear and before it slid down into the grass again touched his cheek with a cold friendly remote tongue. (82)

Scobie's experience of greatest happiness, coming when his wife is far away and just before his first moments alone with Helen Rolt, is described as "being in darkness, alone, with the rain falling, without love or pity" (142). But this is a rare and short-lived moment in his life.

Scobie's activities move with devastating rigor to a complex situation from which suicide seems to him the only "responsible" escape. At the beginning of the novel his ambitious and incessantly whining wife looks forward only to his promotion from Deputy Commissioner to Commissioner of Police and to their eventual retirement far away from West Africa. When he is passed over for promotion, Louise begs him to send her away on a vacation. Unable to afford the passage, Scobie is finally driven through pity for his wife to borrow the money from Yusef, a Syrian in very bad repute with the English and suspected to be a diamond smuggler working against the English cause in the war. With Louise away and with the unprepossessing and unprotected Helen Rolt recuperating in his village from the shipwreck, Scobie succumbs to her ugliness and commits adultery. Louise, who unknown to Scobie has heard of his infidelity, returns, and Scobie finds himself in the impossible situation of a responsibility to the needs and sensibilities of both Louise, to whom he has made a marriage vow, and Helen, to whom he has promised unending care. He is unable to follow Yusef's advice as a solution to his problem: "The way is not to care a damn, Major Scobie. You say to each of them, 'I do not care a damn. I sleep with whom I please. You take me or leave me. I do not care a damn.' They always take you, Major Scobie" (270). Scobie can follow only his own counsel, which leads to suicide.

One of the paradoxes of Scobie's situation is that his every departure from the tenets of conventional morality and religion is motivated by a tender heart. By the time of Louise's return his pity for a Portuguese sea captain has led him, against the urgent demands of his official position, to destroy some evidence which might indict the captain; his pity for his wife has led him to compromise himself into borrowing money from Yusef, a suspected enemy of his government; and his pity for Helen Rolt has led him to commit adultery with her. But his pity reduces him to more than an infidelity to his government and his wife; it makes for at least a seeming desertion of God himself. In his effort to put Helen at rest regarding his devotion to her, he writes her that he loves her *"more than God I think"* (196); and assuring her that he will always be at her call, he reflects, " 'God can wait . . .: how can one love God at the expense of one of his creatures?' " (203)

With Louise's return he becomes even more embroiled in his desperate situation. His wife's first step is to try to persuade him to go to Mass. In the Roman Catholic faith, a person must confess his sins and be absolved of them by the priest before he can properly partake of the Eucharist, a fact which convinces Louise that her husband will take Communion only if he is truly repentant of his adultery. Scobie goes to the confessional, but realizing that he cannot truthfully promise God that he will not be alone with Helen again, he is unable to give evidence of the contriteness of heart which is the indispensable preliminary to absolution. His particular kind of integrity is expressed in his thought, "I am cheating human beings every day I live, I am not going to try to cheat myself or God" (244). But if he cannot grieve Helen by depriving her of his company, he cannot grieve Louise by not partaking of the Communion. Thus caught between his compassion for

Louise and his compassion for Helen, he chooses the only way out, the terrible sin of eating at the Lord's table with mortal sin on his soul. Scobie, familiar enough with Catholic doctrine to realize the enormity of his action, tells Helen that such a Communion is " 'like the Black Mass, the man who steals the sacrament to desecrate it. It's striking God when he's down—in my power' " (232). And as he approaches the Mass, he becomes convinced that he is an even greater sinner than the celebrants of a Black Mass:

> Those ruined priests who presided at a Black Mass, consecrating the Host over the naked body of a woman, consuming God in an absurd and horrifying ritual, were at least performing the act of damnation with an emotion larger than human love: they were doing it from hate of God or some odd perverse devotion to God's enemy. But he had no love of evil or hate of God: how was he to hate this God who of His own accord was surrendering Himself into his power? He was desecrating God because he loved a woman—was it even love, or was it just a feeling of pity and responsibility? (247-248)

Whatever it was, his thoughts of his future desecrations of the Mass bring "a sudden picture before his eyes of a bleeding face, of eyes closed by the continuous shower of blows: the punch-drunk head of God reeling sideways." (264)

Always at the heart of Scobie's actions, at the heart of the matter, is his pity, his all-encompassing sense of compassion and responsibility for the wretched sojourners of this earth. His actions to him add up to more than dereliction of duty, marital infidelity, and desecration of God;

for he has a sense that his love for others, leading as it may to his own damnation, may lead also to a peace for others who, but for him, might have been deprived of it. As the wafer of bread, the very Body of the Lord, is about to be consumed, he prays, " 'O God, I offer up my damnation to you. Take it. Use it for them.' " (250)

It is ironic that Louise at one point in the novel says to one of the other characters, " 'We don't *die* for love, . . . except, of course, in books' " (238), for Scobie's peculiar kind of love for others does bring him to suicide. He is convinced that a person's death sometimes brings peace to his survivors, even to those who love him, for they are thus relieved of any sense of responsibility to him. When he realizes that his own life, despite his manifold efforts to solace both Louise and Helen, can now bring them only misery, he prays, " 'O God, give me death before I give them unhappiness' " (206). And as Helen offers to give him up, he can think only of how his death would bring her freedom and forgetfulness of him (281). Most explicitly are his thoughts expressed in his dialogue with God, to whom Scobie refuses to entrust the responsibility for his own actions:

"No. I don't trust you. I love you, but I've never trusted you. If you made me, you made this feeling of responsibility that I've always carried about like a sack of bricks. I'm not a policeman for nothing—responsible for order, for seeing justice is done. There was no other profession for a man of my kind. I can't shift my responsibility to you. If I could, I would be someone else. I can't make one of them suffer so as to save myself. I'm responsible and I'll see it through the only way I can. A

sick man's death means to them only a short suffering—
everybody has to die. We are all of us resigned to death:
it's life we aren't resigned to." (290)

And so with his customary care he prepares for the
perfect suicide. The pretension that he is stricken with
angina, the harboring of the fatal evipan tablets, the false
diary entries designed to persuade later readers that he had
no anticipation of death—all these are to convince his
survivors that his death was a natural one. He wishes to
carry out his final responsibility well, to avert the suspicion
of the life insurance company, to save Helen from a sense
of guilt, to preserve Louise from the horror of her conviction that suicide incurs absolute damnation. In short, he
dies as he has lived; his last words are " 'Dear God, I
love. . . .' " (299)

A man with Scobie's peculiar and unbending sense of
responsibility must always carry within himself that germ
and raw material of suicide—despair. As Scobie realizes
early in the novel, "despair is the price one pays for setting
oneself an impossible aim" (61), and no one can dispute
the impossibility of Scobie's aim—to carry the burden of
the world's suffering on his own shoulders, unwilling to
share it with God. At the same time, Scobie's ultimate
misery seems to be the answer to one of his most unselfish
and passionate prayers. As he looked down at the pain-
racked body of a six-year-old girl, one of the victims of the
shipwreck, he had prayed, " 'Father, give her peace. Take
away my peace for ever, but give her peace' " (130). The
girl died, and Scobie went on from misery to misery.

In the epilogic conversation between Louise and the

Catholic priest Father Rank, there is speculation about Scobie's ultimate destiny. To Louise, who takes Catholic teaching at its word, her husband is damned. To Father Rank, on whose visage Graham Greene's seems finally to be superimposed, the matter is not so easily decided, is, in fact, a mystery hidden from man and from any institution. The Church may know its dogma, but " 'it doesn't know what goes on in a single human heart,' " and, Father Rank goes on, " 'I think, from what I saw of him, that he really loved God.' " (306)

II

When a Pharisee asks Jesus for the greatest of all the commandments, his answer combines two Old Testament verses, Deuteronomy 6:5 and Leviticus 19:18: " 'You shall love the Lord your God with all your heart, and with all your soul, and with all your mind. This is the great and first commandment. And a second is like it, You shall love your neighbor as yourself. On these two commandments depend all the law and the prophets' " (Matthew 22:37-40). The biblical assumption is that the two commandments go hand in hand and that to follow either one is necessarily to follow the other as well. If any distinction whatsoever of precedent were to be made, the order in which the commandments are given should be noted, as well as the emphasis on *all* in the first one. If a situation occurred in which the two commandments were in any way contradictory—and it is doubtful that biblical thought would ever admit such a contradiction possible, then man's love for God is to take precedence over his love for man.

The greatest Old Testament story of man's love for and trust in God is found in Abraham's near sacrifice of Isaac. Abraham's horrible dilemma could hardly be drawn more extravagantly. Isaac, the son of Abraham's one hundredth year and of Sarah's long-barren womb, was the promised one who was to carry on the seed of his father, peopling the world with a chosen people as numerous as the dust particles of the earth or as the stars of the heavens. Yet when Isaac was still a young boy there spoke, incredibly, the voice of God: " 'Take your son, your only son Isaac, whom you love, and go to the land of Moriah, and offer him there as a burnt offering upon one of the mountains of which I shall tell you' " (Genesis 22:2). It is tempting to think of the many reactions which Abraham might have had to these terrifying words. We would not be too surprised if he had not believed his ears; how could this be the voice of the One who had ordained that the generations of his chosen ones would be carried on through Isaac? Or perhaps God was confused or was suffering from a temporary loss of memory; he might even live to regret it if Abraham carried out his foolish command. Abraham might have gone to Sarah or to some of his friends, telling them tearfully of the Lord's words and apologetically insisting that the whole plan was Jahweh's, not his—otherwise he would be looked upon as an insane murderer rather than one faithfully following an inexplicable command. He might at the least have practiced delaying tactics, living out a few additional precious days with his son. But Abraham did none of these things, and the narration of that harrowing trip to the land of Moriah is well known. He rose up early the next morning, saddled his ass, took two of his young men—and his son—with him, cut the wood for the sacrificial fire, and went on his way to Moriah. Nearing the designated mountain on the third day, he bade the young men to wait, and went on with Isaac to the place of worship, with Isaac bearing the wood on which he was to be sacrificed and Abraham carrying the torch to light the fire and the knife to prepare the sacrifice. There followed the painful dialogue between father and son: " 'My father!'. . . 'Here am I, my son.'. . . 'Behold, the fire and the wood; but where is the lamb for a burnt offering?'. . . 'God will provide himself the lamb for a burnt offering, my son' " (Genesis 22:7-9). And God did, and in the form of the lamb caught in a thicket. Certainly no man, except Jesus, has ever shown such absolute devotion for God. And it would be a false argument to suggest that Abraham did not love Isaac as he loved himself; he loved his son more than himself and would gladly have laid down his own life for him. Nowhere in the Old Testament do we find such perfect obedience to the two commandments which Jesus declared the greatest of all.

The experience of the prophet Hosea is also of considerable importance in any discussion of the biblical concept of love. Though interpretations of the early chapters of the Book of Hosea differ, it would seem that Gomer, Hosea's wife, deserts him and turns to harlotry, perhaps to some form of cultic prostitution practiced in that day. She is later found by her husband wretched and for sale in a slave market. A man's usual reaction to such a situation might be to enjoy a moment of vengeance toward the one who had deserted him, to taunt her, or, at best, to purchase her freedom and then abandon her. But the word of the Lord comes to Hosea, saying, " 'Go again, love a woman who is beloved of a paramour and is an adulteress; even as the Lord loves the people of Israel, though they turn to other gods and love cakes of raisins' " (3:1), and Hosea redeems his wife, and they re-establish their loving relationship. The analogy between God's relationship to man and man's proper relationship to man is made clear. Israel, child and bride of Jahweh, has also been unfaithful, has prostituted herself to false gods, but Israel's harlotry does not cause God to abandon her. His love is so great that he is always willing and indeed eager to redeem his children or wives, and Hosea learns and practices the commandment later given by Jesus to his disciples, " 'that you love one another as I have loved you' " (John 15:12). Hosea's forgiving mercy toward Gomer is like that of Jahweh toward Israel.

In his answer to one of the Pharisees Jesus sums up the message of the Old Testament in the assertion that man should love God with his whole heart and should love his neighbor as himself, commandments which seem to have been grasped with such fullness by Abraham and Hosea. And, as has just been remarked, Jesus complements these commandments with what he calls a "new commandment" in John 13:34 and repeats in John 15:12-14: " 'This is my commandment, that you love one another as I have loved you. Greater love has no man than this, that a man lay down his life for his friends. You are my friends if you do what I command you.' " It is important to know just how Jesus or God has loved man, for it is only through knowing this that man may come to know how to love other men. God's love for man is of a nature which induced Him to give his only Son in death and which induced the Son to accept death. The whole pattern of Christ's life is the pattern of God's kind of love, and perhaps the most striking characteristic of this love is that it is poured upon those who cannot be said to be intrinsically lovable. When the Pharisees reprove Jesus for eating with sinners, he makes clear that they are the very objects of his ministry: " 'Those who are well have no need of a physician, but those who are sick; I came not to call the righteous, but sinners' " (Mark 2:17). The righteous would have no need of a redeemer, and the self-righteous, to whom Jesus is directing his remarks, would have no realization of their need and would consequently not turn to him for their salvation. And he points out to those who would follow him that the love which is the source of his ministry is one which serves others, not which would be served by them: " '. . . whoever would be great among you must be your servant, and whoever would be first among you must be slave of all. For the Son of man also came not to be served but to serve, and to give his life as a ransom for many.' " (Mark 10:44-45)

It is man's natural impulse to love the lovable, that is to say, to love those people whose measure of virtue and beauty serves to magnetize the beholder. Man as a rule loves those who may be of some benefit to him, those who possess something which he desires, or those whose company is pleasurable. Such a love, sometimes called "eros," is not to be confused with a purely sexual eroticism, but is the love which a man may have for his wife, his children, his best friends, or for God Himself. It is what the average person usually means by the word "love." It is not extended to those who are, to the loving one, unattractive or evil; it certainly does not encompass one's enemies, a fact which does not go unnoticed in the Sermon on the Mount. But "eros" is not God's kind of love for man; the perfection which is God would hardly turn to man for his delight in the virtuous or the beautiful. God's love is called "agape," and it is dramatized throughout the Bible, above all in the life, death, and resurrection of Christ. It is no respecter of persons, falling as it does on the evil and the good, the just and the unjust; it seeks nothing for itself. This, according to Christ's new commandment, is the proper pattern for man's love for man.

An understanding of Paul's hymn to love in the thirteenth chapter of First Corinthians depends upon an understanding of the nature of God's love. What sense, for example, can be made of the third verse—"If I give away all I have, and if I deliver my body to be burned, but have not love, I gain nothing"—without an understanding of "agape"? In reading this verse we recall immediately the rich young man, one who had observed God's commandments, who came to Jesus and asked how he might inherit eternal life. "You lack one thing," Jesus replied; "go, sell what you have, and give to the poor, and you will have treasure in heaven; and come, follow me" (Mark 10:21). Was he not told that to give away all he had was to gain the kingdom of Heaven, and does this not seem a contradiction to Paul's statement? And what about the long role of martyrs who gave their bodies to be burned? Did their action avail them nothing? The only answer is that one can give away all he has or even suffer martyrdom for the wrong reason, that is, for any reason other than the impulse of agape. The rich young man *could* have given away all he had and still not followed Jesus, for a man *can* be charitable simply in hopes of personal gain or of high repute. And, as T. S. Eliot's Thomas Becket discovered, a man *can* seek martyrdom for the wrong reason, can give up his life not in loving service of God and man but in hope of reward. The ultimate test of any human action is whether it was occasioned by man's surrender of himself in love to others; the ultimate test of a man's sanctity is his possession of the gift of agape, the gift to love others as God loves him.

It can be said further that a person is not really alive in a Christian sense unless he does possess this gift, and it is one of the paradoxes of Christian thought that death precedes life, not life death. The man conceived in sin is born dead, and as Jesus tells Nicodemus in the third chapter of the Fourth Gospel, a man must be born anew if he would see the kingdom of God; to be born of the flesh is death, but to be born of the Spirit is life. There is only one true mark of life, and that is the possession of a love which is God's love: "We know that we have passed out of death into life, because we love the brethren. He who does not love remains in death. Any one who hates his brother is a murderer, and you know that no murderer has eternal life abiding in him. By this we know love, that he laid down his life for us; and we ought to lay down our lives for the brethren" (I John 3:14-16). There could be no more explicit imperative in the Christian life.

It is left to Paul to make the most incredible statement of all about the nature of man's love, a statement perhaps beyond the grasp of the human imagination. He is grieving that his people, the Israelites, have, through their blindness to the light of Christ, refused to accept him as their savior, and Paul expresses a wish which has no parallel in the biblical text; it goes even beyond a willingness to lay down one's life for his friends—it exposes a willingness to be cut off from God eternally if, through his damnation, his beloved people may be saved: "For I could wish that I myself were accursed and cut off from Christ for the sake of my brethren, my kinsmen by race" (Romans 9:3). Is this a godly extension of "greater love has no man," or is it sheer madness?

III

What is the final implication of *The Heart of the Matter* in regard to the life and the death of Scobie? Is the reader to conclude that Scobie's sins effect his eternal damnation or that his peculiar kind of love marks him as an adopted son of God? Though the answer to these questions may not be clear, the questions are clearly put and the issue itself is clearly drawn, perhaps too clearly drawn, for the action of the novel does at times seem contrived. The reader occasionally questions the credibility of Scobie's character, wondering if his actions always spring from himself or are sometimes superimposed by the too evident hand of the author. Graham Greene would seem to be asking himself how many sins he could place upon Scobie without bringing the reader to giving him up as absolutely lost.

Scobie consciously sets out to follow what may be regarded as a near paraphrase of the "new commandment" of Christ: to "love human beings nearly as God loved them." Unable to believe in a "God who was not human enough to love what he had created" (125), Scobie takes upon himself the burden of this love, directed particularly toward those who are unloved by others. When Helen Rolt remarks rather cuttingly that she thinks " 'he only likes the sick' " (209), one remembers Christ's words to the Pharisees that the well need no physician. And when we note the desperate quality of Scobie's love, we recall his own thought of "how desperately God must love" (235). What is perhaps most startling about Scobie's passion is his willingness to offer up his own damnation as a sacrifice for others; and his prayers that he may lose his peace forever if only the painfully dying young girl may gain peace, and that he may die before he brings further unhappiness to Louise and Helen. His thought early in the novel—"It's terrible the way prayer is answered" (100)—bears a fine irony. I know of no other character in fiction who tries actually to carry out Paul's expressed willingness to be cut off from Christ for the sake of his brethren.

One of the novel's most fascinating problems is whether Scobie is to be viewed as a person who gives his life as a ransom for others, or as a person guilty of the most outlandish pride. In the scene in which he prays for the peace of the girl even at the expense of his own peace, we are told that sweat "broke out on his hands," and "poured down his face" (130), and are carried back to the Lucan account of Christ's prayer at Gethsemane, to His willingness to drink the bitter cup for others, and to the agonized sweat falling like drops of blood to the ground (Luke 22:42-44). And when Scobie, in a state of mortal sin, prays that some miracle may preserve him from the damnation of receiving the Eucharist, he reasons that God did not perform a miracle to save himself on the Cross and thinks: "I am the Cross . . . : He will never speak the word to save Himself from the Cross, but if only wood were made so that it didn't feel, if only the nails were senseless as people believe" (249). It even occurs to him as he contemplates suicide that "Christ had not been murdered: you couldn't murder God: Christ had killed himself: he had hanged himself on the Cross. . . ." (207)

Does all this add up to humility or to arrogant pride? Scobie constantly rejects the temptation to put his own soul first. "One should look after one's own soul at whatever cost to another," he thinks, "and that's what I can't do, what I shall never be able to do" (199). And later he prays: " 'Make me put my own soul first. Give me trust in your mercy to the one I abandon' " (243-244). But it is precisely this trust which Scobie lacks. In his dialogue with God about his fear of bringing suffering to Louise or Helen, God says to him, "One of them will suffer, but can't you trust me to see that the suffering isn't too great?" (290). Scobie must answer "No." Can a person who lacks trust in

God, who deserts his professional duty, who commits both adultery and suicide be viewed as redeemed? The answer would seem to be evident, but each time the reader is ready to pronounce it, he is brought back to a consideration of Scobie's intentions, to the fact that he gives his life "to love human beings nearly as God loved them," even though his passionate effort leads him into some very strange byways seldom permitted in any conventional view of morality or religion.

The Heart of the Matter is, I think, a tremendous tour de force whose theme might be summed up in some such paraphrase as the following: "If I lie and desert my duty, and if I commit adultery and suicide, and if I lack trust in God, but have love, I gain the Kingdom." If one were to come upon the paraphrase apart from the novel, it would seem absurd; but if a reading of the novel brings to the paraphrase a measure of credibility, then the novel enjoys some measure of success. Graham Greene would seem to be asserting that judgment must be left to God, and that however sinful a person's actions may appear, no one can know how that person stands in the eyes of God; a complementary argument might be made that however virtuous a person's actions may appear no one can know how he stands in God's eyes. Not even the Church can pass any ultimate judgment, strive as it may to know God's will and to guide its flock in the light of that will. Scobie is Greene's spokesman when he tells Helen that " '. . . against all the teaching of the Church, one has the conviction that love— any kind of love—does deserve a bit of mercy. One will pay, of course, pay terribly, but I don't believe one will pay for ever. Perhaps one will be given time before one dies . . .'" (231). The novel's concluding scene, the conversation between Louise and Father Rank, reads almost in terms of a morality play with Louise in the role of Conventional Morality and the priest in that of Divine Compassion. The important things in a man's life, says Divine Compassion, are his virtues, not his sins. He goes on to suggest to Conventional Morality that the human imagination cannot grasp the immensity of God's mercy and that not even the Church can see to the very bottom of a human heart.

In fact, much of the novel may be read as a morality play, a genre in which the author does come closer to the puppeteer than he may properly come in other forms of literature. If Scobie is not always a convincing three-dimensional character, if Greene's hand is too clearly envisaged behind the scenes, perhaps the justification lies in the novel's approach to the morality play genre.

In terms of the novel Scobie is, I think, saved, and the measure of Greene's success must lie in the measure in which he is able to persuade the reader of the paradox that Scobie, despite the dimensions of his sins, has gained the peace which he so passionately desired but which he was, nevertheless, willing to surrender if his surrender might bring peace to others. It is true that Scobie's most careful efforts fail to bring peace to Helen, who passively abandons herself to the immature and irresponsible Bagster, or to Louise, who, it is implied, will eventually marry the weak and self-pious Wilson. Perhaps there lies in the novel the final suggestion that Scobie must in death, as he should have done in life, entrust to God the welfare of those whom he tried most to solace, those who do not yet feel in their hearts the love for God and the love or compassion for man which possessed Scobie.

6.

THE THEME OF THE REMNANT:

Ignazio Silone's *A Handful of Blackberries*

> *He has showed you, O man, what is good;*
> *and what does the Lord require of you*
> *but to do justice, and to love kindness,*
> *and to walk humbly with your God?* (Micah 6:8)

I

"I'm laughing because I've got a seat," said Alfredo. "And you're wrong not to laugh, since you've got one too. You're entitled to laugh. But you never did have any sense of solidarity." (9)*

Toward the beginning of Ignazio Silone's *A Handful of Blackberries*, a crowded bus stopped by the Café Mazzini to take on new passengers. One of them, a woman, angrily demanding that the driver give her a seat, became even more irate when the seated passengers laughed at the driver's request to see where it was written on her ticket that she

---

* In this chapter, all excerpts from *A Handful of Blackberries* by Ignazio Silone are used by the permission of the publisher, Harper & Brothers, New York. Darina Silone was the translator. Page references are to the Harper & Brothers edition, 1953.

158

had a right to be seated. " 'Listen,' " said an old woman to her through the window, " 'if you happened to have a seat, wouldn't you laugh yourself? Well, then!' " (9) When Alfredo's laughter was challenged by Rocco, he gave the reply, quoted above, which serves as a kind of microcosm for the entire novel.

Alfredo Esposito had spent his life's energy in his rural Italian valley trying to make certain that he always had a seat and always maintained a solidarity with those in power. Under the previous Fascist regime he had so ingratiated himself with Mussolini that he was appointed municipal tax collector, a post which had served him well: after paying off his debts and building himself a villa, he had turned to works of charity for those less fortunate. And when the Fascists surrendered their seats to the Liberation Committee and the Communist Party, Alfredo was considerably relieved that the new rulers viewed him as a useful cohort and accepted his services rather than liquidating him. As Filomena, the café waitress, told him twice, " 'you're back in the saddle again' " (14, 16). Alfredo had great confidence in the solidarity of whatever the ruling hierarchy happened to be; he gravitated with unfailing precision toward the seated ones, those in power.

The thesis of Silone's novel is that power corrupts and that any organization which gains some measure of it forgets quickly its early ideals and becomes, if not self-defeating, at least destructive of those human beings whom it originally set out to rescue from oppression. Silone's spokesman is Rocco de Donatis, central character of the book and a man whose life finds its foil in Alfredo. Rocco is, like the Socrates of Plato's *Gorgias*, a man who, while preferring to live in a world free from injustice, would nevertheless rather suffer injustice than be unjust. He would put no premium on a seat in the bus, a pew in the Church, or a post in the Party, because he knew that when a persecuted being finally routs his persecutors, he is likely to assume the role of persecutor. Alfredo chose to persecute, Rocco to be persecuted. Indeed, each of the novel's main characters falls into one of two general groups: (1) the persecutors, those who in their cowardliness and insecurity wish to remain in the saddle, to bask in the favor and protection of the most predominant and powerful organization; (2) the persecuted, those who love justice more than they fear power. Rocco and his friends gather into a community bent upon following God's will as it is revealed to them, upon remaining faithful to God and to each other, whatever the cost. Their appointed end on this earth is to form a community of love for the succoring of the oppressed.

Rocco's consuming passion for justice and his conviction that an institution's sense of justice is in inverse proportion to its successful growth caused him to break with the two predominant institutions of his place and day—the Roman Catholic Church and the Communist Party. As a youth Rocco seemed headed for the priesthood. But one morning as he was attending Mass at the parish church in La Fornace, he suddenly realized that the other parishioners were in no way possessed by the profound mystery of the Sacrament; in fact, they were possessed by nothing. Their souls, Rocco told his companion, " 'are neither hot nor cold. It was of them that the Eternal Father spoke when He said: "Because thou art lukewarm and neither hot nor cold, I will spew thee out of My mouth." Don't they nauseate you?'" (77). Rocco left the church during the Mass, never to attend another service. He gave up the Church not only because of the thoughtless and mechanical participation of its members, but also because of the Church's own failure to feed its sheep and to exert benefits where they were most needed: "My choice of the poor as comrades was and still remains the most important act of my life. Because of them I left the Church, gave up my thoughts of the priesthood, hastened my mother's death." (286)

It is ironic, in view of subsequent events, that Marxist doctrine was responsible for Rocco's break with the Church. We are told that "politics . . . , like some violent disease, took hold of Rocco" (76). If there was no passion in the Church, if the priests had no real care for the poor, then perhaps an idealistic secular system would bring about the alleviation of suffering and injustice which he sought; if a divine institution had lost the intensity and righteousness which would work toward a good worldly order, perhaps a secular institution would carry out the Lord's will. Rocco could possibly exert his priestly function more effectively through the framework of the Party than through that of the Church. He threw himself eagerly into the work of the Party, acquitting himself with success and earning the respect of his colleagues. But a mission to Russia and Poland enabled him to see the organization at close range, and he came to the terrible realization that his earlier dreams of the panacea of Marxism bore little relationship to the

actual workings of the Party. In Warsaw he had met a
former acquaintance, a girl who had left a promising medi-
cal career to work in a Moscow publishing house at the
Party's command; he hardly recognized her, changed as
she had been through a torturous confinement by the Communists—such unmistakable evidence of their brutality was
the last blow to his dream of their good will. The very
quality which attracted Alfredo to the Party was that which
led Rocco to abandon it as he had earlier abandoned the
Church: "'. . . the Party of today is not what it used to be.
It was a Party of the persecuted, now it is a party of persecutors. It was a gathering of young, free, unbiased men; it
has become a barracks, a police headquarters. At its least
hateful, it's an administration.'" (145)

The primary action of *A Handful of Blackberries* takes
place in an isolated rural valley in Italy shortly after the
fall of Mussolini, but the source of its dramatic conflict
goes well beyond such spatial and temporal boundaries: it is
the conflict between wealthy oppressors and poor oppressed.
In terms of the novel, the oppressors are the landowning
Tarocchi family, who have long controlled virtually all
aspects—political, economic, and religious—of their valley;
the oppressed are the poor shepherds, farmers, and laborers
whose holdings, of whatever nature they may be, have
always been exceedingly meager. Since the Tarocchi control the courts, the peasants who seek legal recourse against
injustice find that an appeal to law brings only greater injustice. The one great weapon that the peasants have is the
indomitable spirit of their few courageous leaders, a spirit
symbolized by a mysterious trumpet: "'The trumpet used

to be sounded to call together the landless peasants whenever there was cause. And every time the gentry, especially the Tarocchi, would be filled with terror and bewilderment; it was their nightmare. On certain evenings . . . it seemed the Day of Judgment and the Last Trumpet' " (58). When Lazzaro and Martino, leaders of the rebellious peasants, refused to divulge the whereabouts of the trumpet to the armed and anxious officials, they were banished from the valley. When Rocco discovered that the members of the Church were those who cowered before the injustice surrounding them and that the priests raised no dissenting voice, he left the Church, eager to serve those who preached a gospel of freedom, the Marxists. But if neither the pre-Fascist nor the Fascist regime had brought freedom to the valley, he was to learn that the Communist Party was to do no better. In fact, during the course of the novel, the Party officials and the Tarocchi come to seek a mutually profitable alliance: in return for some of the Tarocchi property, the officials are willing to protect the wealthy family, maintaining them in their splendor to the continued impoverishment of the peasants.

The bitter wisdom that comes to Rocco is that an organization's success is a society's failure, that organization or institutionalism is intrinsically corrupt because the organizers lose sight of their original ideals as soon as they accomplish their purpose of freeing themselves from a former organization's power. As Rocco said, the Party in its first stages was made up of "young, free, unbiased" men who sought to right the inequalities fostered by a decadent political and a decadent religious order. But once the young men climbed into the saddle, they did not change the moral and ethical situation so much as they replaced one set of oppressors by another.

One of the ironies of the novel is that the Party, hostile as it was to the Church, to a great extent took over the organizational structure of the Church and the very mechanisms which had served it well in the role of oppressor. One of Alfredo's first ingenious moves when he joined the Communists was "the establishment of an Indulgence Office, as one of the chief organs of the Party to help rehabilitate capitalists and other important personages compromised by their association with the defunct regime. The office would determine the sum to be paid in each case, taking into account the gravity of the errors committed and the financial resources of the penitent" (18). The Party leaflets were referred to as "the revelation of the new faith" (34). Deviants from the Party line took their place with those who challenged the dogma of the Church as "heretics" (116). The Party found solace in relics, two of which consisted of "a little bag of rubble from the city of Stalingrad and a handkerchief stained with the blood of a heroic partisan" (117). The main items in the Communist library were copies of the " 'Official Party Catechism, in questions and answers, duly authorized and brought up to date.' " (118)

The Church and the Party showed relationships in terms not only of structure and procedure but also of the quality of their respective priesthoods. Both priests and Party officials were more concerned with their own welfare than with that of those whom they were presumed to serve. Don

Guistino Tarocchi, late parish priest of San Luca, bore many of the endearing characteristics of some of Chaucer's Canterbury pilgrims. Like Chaucer's Monk, he was a great hunter, tending to his parish only in the winter and spending the other seasons enjoying the hunt with his horse, double-barreled gun, and dogs. And like Chaucer's Friar, he was well-skilled in the art of seduction. He refused to wear trousers under his cassock because, as he said, " 'They would get in the way' " (79). Whereas the Friar arranged suitable marriages for the victims of his ardor, Don Guistino, an expert in gynecology, served as midwife for his intimate friends. Being a Tarocchi, he was not forced to pay much heed to his Bishop's complaints. And then there was the parish priest Don Constantino, who commended himself to Mussolini during the Ethiopian War by preaching a series of sermons on " 'The Man of Providence and the Holy War against the *Negus*' " (103), and by sanctifying the use of poison gas, so long of course as it was used to the glory of the "One True Church" (103). The eagerness of the Party members to form a coalition with the Tarocchi family is sufficient indication that they too were not above disloyalty to the poor whose cause their Party had originally espoused. Nor should we forget that wonderful marriage of the worst features of Church and Party, brought together under the banner of the Red Churchwomen, one of whose members had received a visit from Jesus: "The Divine Saviour had appeared to her clad in a long red robe. He did not utter a word, but He showed her His heart, on which the new symbols of the hammer and sickle were engraved in gold" (226). The same member fretfully wondered if, on the day of Resurrection, she could carry her Party membership card with her into heaven.

If Rocco had been, to his credit, a misfit in the Party, then the priest Don Nicola, his friend since high school days, was a misfit in the Church. As Lazzaro told them, " 'One of you is never done making trouble for the Party and the other is a thorn in the side of his Bishop' " (299). Don Nicola did not, like Rocco, leave the Church, but within the Church he paid less attention to dogma than to the human beings under his care. His actions bore even more eloquent testimony to his goodness than the words which show the springs of his conduct: " 'Love is the best Christian catechism. For the rest, faith is a matter of Grace' " (181). It was he who helped nurture the Jewish orphan Stella, respected her faith, nursed her back to life during her crucial heart-sickness, and helped arrange for her marriage to Rocco. And it was he who recognized that Martino, not a member of the Church, was " 'perhaps [his] best parishioner' " (73). In short, he was one of the few who were able to remain true to themselves and to the doctrine of love while remaining within the framework of an institution.

The other saints in the novel had to live their lives without benefit of Church or Party. There was Martino (who, by the way, had been barred from the local church because the priest's sister had "ruled that out of respect to God's house she would no longer tolerate people coming to church barefoot" (91)); this courageous rebel willingly risked his life to minister to his injured father, longingly awaited

" 'the Kingdom of God on earth' " (75), and twice suffered banishment from his valley because of his love for his fellows. There was Lazzaro, who received a call from God in the form of a ruthlessly murdered young girl dying in his arms after having been trampled by a cavalry charge of the *carabinieri* against the day laborers; the occasion awakened his senses of justice and love. It was he who probably would have been called an apostle had he lived in the days of Christ (298), and it was he of whom Don Nicola said, " 'the rustic saints that evangelized our valleys and accepted martyrdom were of the same species' " (301). And there was, of course, Rocco, who, again according to Don Nicola, " 'was the object of the clearest call from God that I have ever witnessed. . . . But although he did not obey his vocation he has constantly demanded from secular life the absolute quality that he could have found only in a monastery' " (84). It was his fidelity to God's call which finally made it impossible for him to speak in behalf of the Party. When questioned by the Communist Oscar about his refusal to speak, he answered that he suffered from a peculiar ailment when he was called upon to speak for the Party: " 'You see, while I was speaking, I could hear my own voice as though it belonged to someone else. I was listening to someone else's oratory.' " And when Oscar asked if he ever experienced this difficulty under other circumstances, he replied, " 'It never happens when I'm saying what I think' " (122). The expression of what he thought grew out of a spirit which viewed all men as brothers, not out of a rigid ideology which placed either Party or self-interest above the second great commandment. Rocco could not long remain within the discipline of an organization whose guiding principle is well expressed by one of its officials: " 'You know the infallible criterion of the Party: anything that harms Russia is false.' " (218)

To what can such independent spirits as Rocco and Stella, Lazzaro and Martino, and Don Nicola look forward? They can joyfully anticipate what Rocco calls, in the last chapter of the novel, " 'the future Liberation.' " It may come " 'next year, or sixty or even two thousand years from now,' " and when it does come it will be both a civic and a religious occasion, transforming the whole of man's life. The future hope is expressed in more colloquial and colorful language by the old shepherd Massimiliano:

> "There'll always be someone that refuses to sell his soul for a handful of beans and a piece of cheese. . . . And at the very end, when the worms think they've won, there'll come the angel. He'll take the trumpet from its hiding place and he'll sound it full blast and he'll wake even the dead. I'd like to see you then, craven maggots that you are; I'd like to see if you're able to snatch the trumpet from the angel's hands. Aha, I'd like to see you then."
> (311)

The same hope is voiced more tenderly and charitably through the Christlike Lazzaro's vision of faith. Stella asks him at the very end of the novel if there is any meaning in life's activities. " 'Haven't you ever thought,' said Lazzaro, 'that there's something guiding the movement of the ants underground and the flight of birds from one continent to another?' " Stella points out, however, that not all of them make a safe voyage, that some do not have the strength or the courage to reach their destination. Lazzaro agrees, and, remembering the innocent girl who died in his arms, he says, " 'On the way, there are some that get trampled and killed by the horses' hooves.' " But the reader must remember that out of the child's death sprang the new spirit of Lazzaro, and that out of the new spirit came the trumpet which summons all the dispossessed to carry on until some day, maybe "next year, or sixty or even two thousand years from now," when the blood of all the innocents will effect the redemption of the righteous.

II

"For you are a people holy to the Lord your God; the Lord your God has chosen you to be a people for his own possession, out of all the peoples that are on the face of the earth. . . .

"And because you hearken to these ordinances [God's commandments], and keep and do them, the Lord your God will keep with you the covenant and the steadfast love which he swore to your fathers to keep; he will love you, bless you, and multiply you; he will also bless the fruit of your body and the fruit of your ground, your grain and your wine and your oil, the increase of your cattle and the young of your flock, in the land which he swore to your fathers to give you." (Deuteronomy, 7:6, 12-13)

Moses' words to the Israelites on the way from Egypt to the Promised Land embody two very important Pentateuchal proclamations. One is that the Israelites are the chosen people of Jahweh, who made known his choice in his call to Abram narrated in the twelfth chapter of Genesis.

The other is that the righteous, those who follow the Lord's commandments, will be covered with all kinds of material blessings. But the empirical experience of the Israelites over a number of years modified their concept of God's relationship to his people and of the relationship between righteous action and worldly prosperity. It became evident that if all the descendants of Abraham were chosen, then some of them abrogated their contract with the Lord. Certainly not all the Israelites acted as if they were men of God, and Aaron's making of the golden calf was the archetype for any number of similar idolatrous deeds. If it could be said that not all the "chosen" ones accepted their blessed status, it could also be said that not all the righteous ones received any immediate and material evidence of God's favor, that one could simply not depend upon any unfailing causal relationship between virtue and reward.

The Israelites sometimes forgot that the promise of Jahweh's favor in his covenant with them was contingent upon their obedience and faithfulness; such forgetfulness gave them a false sense of security which frequently led to a dangerous complacency. They looked forward to the Day of the Lord on which their enemies would be routed and they would be placed on thrones of power and glory, and it was the prophet Amos who first cautioned that the Day of the Lord was to be feared as much as yearned for, that the wrath of God would fall upon the sinning Israelites as well as upon their sinning enemies: "Woe to you who desire the day of the Lord!/Why would you have the day of the Lord?/ It is darkness and not light . . ." (5:18). Amos attempted to impress on the Israelites the fact that the relationship which they bore to Abraham and the careful abiding by the ritual and cultic practices of their religious institution were by no means sufficient to keep them in the Lord's favor. He raised his prophetic voice against the conservative and priestly tradition which sought a salvation by means of the tradition, which seemed to feel that the observation of institutional ceremony was enough to maintain them in their chosen position. The Lord called for justice and righteousness, not sacrifices and burnt offerings:

> "I hate, I despise your feasts,
>> and I take no delight in your solemn assemblies.
> Even though you offer me your burnt offerings and
>> cereal offerings,
>> I will not accept them,
> and the peace offerings of your fatted beasts
>> I will not look upon.
> Take away from me the noise of your songs;
>> to the melody of your harps I will not listen.
> But let justice roll down like waters,
>> and righteousness like an everflowing stream."
>> (Amos 5:21-24)

As Amos continued to proclaim his visions from the Lord, he encountered the opposition of both the civil and the religious powers. Amaziah, the priest of Bethel, after reporting to Jeroboam, king of Israel, that Amos was preaching heretical and discomforting doctrine, warned Amos that he must " 'never again prophesy at Bethel, for it is the king's sanctuary, and it is a temple of the kingdom' " (7:13). Certainly one of the convictions of the Book of Amos is that an Israelite could not depend upon his lineage and his religious institution for salvation.

The prophecy of Jeremiah develops further the idea that not all those bearing a nominal relationship to Jahweh will be saved. Preaching to the men of Judah he warns them not to be deceived by their seeming relationship to the temple: " 'Thus says the Lord of hosts, the God of Israel, Amend your ways and your doings, and I will let you dwell in this place. Do not trust in these deceptive words: 'This is the temple of the Lord, the temple of the Lord, the temple of the Lord' " (7:3-4). The priesthood is rebuked, and it is made clear to them that not all the chosen people will be saved, but rather that a remnant of the faithful will be gathered to carry on the sacred covenant:

> "Woe to the shepherds who destroy and scatter the sheep of my pasture!" says the Lord. Therefore thus says the Lord, the God of Israel, concerning the shepherds who care for my people: "You have scattered my flock, and have driven them away, and you have not attended to them. Behold, I will attend to you for your evil doings, says the Lord. Then I will gather the remnant of my flock out of all the countries where I have driven them, and I will bring them back to their fold, and they shall be fruitful and multiply." (23:1-3)

Jeremiah affirms also that Jahweh will make a new covenant with Israel and Judah,

> ". . . not like the covenant which I made with their fathers when I took them by the hand to bring them out of the land of Egypt, my covenant which they broke, though I was their husband, says the Lord. But this is the covenant which I will make with the house of Israel after those days, says the Lord: I will put my law within them, and I will write it upon their hearts; and I will be their God, and they shall be my people." (31:32-33)

In the course of Old Testament history, then, the view as to who actually constitute the Lord's people changed. Of the many descendants of Abraham, only a remnant would be saved, and their mark of election would be an inward one—the Law would be written on their hearts. At the same time, the concept of virtue rewarded, the belief that there was a mechanical, though providential, system in which a good deed was followed by a concrete reward and an evil one by a concrete punishment was challenged. The classical documents in protest of this view are, as we have seen in earlier chapters, the Book of Job and Second Isaiah, particularly in the Suffering Servant passages. At this time, it is sufficient to say that the lives of some of the prophets, who surely in the biblical view are among the righteous, bear testimony to the fact that acute physical and mental suffering falls upon God's chosen ones. Not only was Amos banished from the temple by the ruling priest. Jeremiah cursed the day that he was born (15:10, 20:14-15); he was beaten by the priest Pashue, "chief officer in the house of the Lord," and then placed in the stocks (20:1-2); he was the laughingstock of his people, the object of mockery, reproach, and derision (20:7-8). In the thirty-sixth chapter of his book we learn that Jeremiah, " 'debarred from going to the house of the Lord,' " sends Baruch there to read the scroll which the prophet had written at the dictation of the Lord. The contents of the scroll were reported to King Jehoiakim, who ordered Jehudi to get the scroll and read it to him; Jehoiakim's reaction to the reading is reported with a nice sense of concrete detail: "As Jehudi read three or four columns, the king would cut them off with a penknife and throw them into the fire in the brazier, until the entire scroll was consumed in the fire that was in the brazier." (Jeremiah 36:23)

We discover in the prophets a very formidable opposition to the status quo of both nation and temple. They promulgated the doctrine of the remnant, they bore living witness to the fact that the Lord's chosen were frequently called upon to suffer for his sake, and they taught that a man's righteousness did not rest securely on his ability to mouth the words, "This is the temple of the Lord, the temple of the Lord, the temple of the Lord." They pointed to a new covenant of the Lord in which Jahweh would engrave the words of the Law on the inner hearts and spirits of his elect.

From the New Testament point of view, the remnant is made up of the followers of Jesus Christ; the Christian people constitute the New Jerusalem. Paul, after referring to the remnant in Old Testament times, affirms that "so too at the present time there is a remnant, chosen by grace" (Romans 11:5), and this is the grace of the Lord Jesus Christ. Jesus himself carries on the prophetic tradition of the Old Testament, and his strictures against the Pharisees are like those of the prophets of Israel and Judah against the priesthood of their day. The Pharisees observe the letter of the Law, tithing " 'mint and dill and cummin,' " but they neglect " 'the weightier matters of the law, justice and mercy and faith' " (Matthew 23:23). They are more intent upon observing the tradition of the elders (including the washing of their hands before meals!) than upon following God's will; Jesus tells them,

"Well did Isaiah prophesy of you hypocrites, as it is written,
'This people honors me with their lips,
but their heart is far from me;
in vain do they worship me,
teaching as doctrines the precepts of men.'
You leave the commandment of God and hold fast the
tradition of men." (Mark 7:6-8)

Jesus also makes clear that God's final judgment upon
men may cause a few surprises, both to those who are over-
confident of God's favor and to those who do not presume
too much upon it. It seems almost an echo of Jeremiah's
comment on those who feel secure if they can repeat, "This
is the temple of the Lord," when Jesus says, " 'Not every
one who says to me, "Lord, Lord," shall enter the kingdom
of heaven, but he who does the will of my Father who is
in heaven' " (Matthew 7:21). And when the faithful cen-
turion with the paralyzed servant lying at home shows
absolute trust in his power, Jesus remarks that he has not
seen such faith in Israel, and that " 'many will come from
east and west and sit at table with Abraham, Isaac, and
Jacob in the kingdom of heaven, while the sons of the
kingdom will be thrown into the outer darkness . . .' "
(Matthew 8:11-12). Perhaps the most striking example of
the teaching that mere words and institutional practices
do not suffice for salvation is the parable of the Last Judgment in the twenty-fifth chapter of Matthew. On the Last
Day the King will summon to him those sheep assembled at
his right hand, telling them that in times of need they fed
him, gave him drink, welcomed him, clothed him, and
visited him. But the righteous ones do not remember any
of these activities, and the King has to explain his words:

" ' "Truly, I say to you, as you did it to one of the least of these my brethren, you did it to me" ' " (25:40). When the King turns to the goats at his left hand and tells them that they must depart into the eternal fire for failing to do the same deeds, they too are puzzled, not remembering having seen the Lord " ' "hungry or thirsty or a stranger or naked or sick or in prison" ' " (25:44), but they are told that they never showed love and mercy to the least of the brethren. Jesus is preaching in parable form essentially the same message as that of the prophet Micah, that the Lord requires man " ' to do justice, and to love kindness,/and to walk humbly with God.' " (Micah 6:8)

The remnant will consist of those persons who follow these requirements of the Lord, who have the Law engraved upon their hearts, and who do not look upon mere verbal professions and outward observances as the sum and substance of God's will for man. The remnant comprises the elect community of God, called upon both to be oppressed and to relieve oppression on earth, and then called to take its place in God's kingdom. Such is the prophetic tradition, one which seems invariably at odds with an established institutionalism whose complacency has occasioned its lifelessness and decay.

III

A Handful of Blackberries, though its story is focused more on the evils of the Communist Party than on those of the Christian church, is nevertheless a severe indictment of them both. They share the disease which seems to be part and parcel of most established institutions, the disease in which the organization, born out of a passionate desire to rectify wrongs and establish justice, devolves from a healthy body viewing itself as a means for accomplishing its noble ideals to an unhealthy one viewing itself as an end in itself. Rocco, before losing his devotion to the Party, once explained one of its central principles to some of its less initiated followers who had locally and independently put into practice the Party's social program: "The more an action resembles something the Party might conceivably do, the more treacherous and vile it is, if performed without the knowledge and against the will of the Party' " (39). And when asked if the Party is not to be found in its program, Rocco replied: " 'The Party is above its program. Do you know what would be the greatest betrayal of all? To carry out the program without the Party' " (40). This dialogue reminds one of a conversation between Jesus and his disciple John. John related that the disciples, seeing a man casting out demons in Jesus' name, had forbidden him to do so because he was not following the disciples; Jesus' answer is a reproval of such parochialism: " 'Do not forbid him; for no one who does a mighty work in my name will be able soon after to speak evil of me. For he that is not against us is for us. For truly, I say to you, whoever gives you a cup of water to drink because you bear the name of Christ, will by no means lose his reward.' " (Mark 9:39-41)

To place any group or institution above the name of Christ is idolatry, the worship of any thing or being other than the One God. One of idolatry's most common objects is the institution, whether it be in religious, political, economic, or any other form. Biblical and Christian history, from Eve's defection to the present time, play innumerable variations on the theme of idolatry, of the constant temptation to worship some form of golden calf. Silone's novel stands within this tradition. Rocco would have made a superb first-generation Christian, as would Don Nicola, Stella, Lazzaro, and Martino. Rocco would never have left the persecuted Church of Peter and Paul, the Church which had to suffer that the will of God might be done. When he realized that the nominal members of the Body of Christ of his day were "lukewarm and neither hot nor cold" and that the clergy, fearful of the power of wealthy landowners and established government, placed their allegiance to the status quo and its support above the shepherding of the sheep whose care Christ had entrusted to Peter in the last chapter of the Fourth Gospel—then he felt called to leave an institution which seemed no longer to be inspired by God's presence, and serve within a framework which seemed to him to be committed to the ideals which the Church had surrendered. The primitive Party had in common with the primitive Church the fact that it was the object of unremitting persecution. We learn that he maintained his devotion to the Party as long as it was persecuted (126), that he viewed the Party as a glorious institution as long as it had to live underground (138), and that one of his most bitter comments about the Party was that " 'for many of our comrades the revolution now consists in taking over the role of persecutors' " (141). The result is that Rocco is left without Church or Party, forced to carry on his life's ideals in company with a few other fearless souls, devoted to love of their fellow men.

The novel would seem to be saying that the man of true faith must always work outside the institutions of his time, unless he happens to be contemporary with an institution which has not yet lost itself in unthinking, mechanical ritual and rigid ideology. Alfredo's damnation was that he always yearned to be in or to remain in the saddle, but both the Bible and Silone demonstrate that God's work has seldom been accomplished from the saddle. The prophetic tradition is a protest against those in the saddle, and we have seen ample evidence that the protesters have taken their places among the persecuted. The dissident voices of Amos and Jeremiah and the other Old Testament prophets find a continuation in the New Testament, where the Acts of the Apostles chronicles the protests of Stephen, Peter, and Paul among others, and narrates colorfully the indignities and tortures to which they were subjected. Paul's most complete account of his own persecution is recorded in the eleventh chapter of Second Corinthians, where he tells us that his witnessing for Christ caused him to be lashed, beaten with rods, stoned, and faced with all manner of hardships. Even more familiar is the journey from the temple, from which the money-changers had been driven, to the Cross. All those against whom the prophetic tradition ranges itself might well heed Isaiah's words:

> Woe to those who decree iniquitous decrees,
>   and the writers who keep writing oppression,
> to turn aside the needy from justice
>   and to rob the poor of my people of their right,
> that widows may be their spoil,
>   and that they may make the fatherless their prey!

What will you do on the day of punishment,
  in the storm which will come from afar?
To whom will you flee for help,
  and where will you leave your wealth?
Nothing remains but to crouch among the prisoners
  or fall among the slain.
For all this his anger is not turned away
  and his hand is stretched out still. (10:1-4)

What solace and hope is there for those who refuse to take a comfortable position in the saddle, preferring to remain on the fringes of, or completely outside, the established institution? Are their voices futile, and is their suffering an end in itself? One of the Old Testament answers to their predicament is, as we have seen, the doctrine of the remnant. Not all the sons of Abraham will be blessed, but only those who keep Jahweh's covenant. They will form a faithful community on earth, bound together by their sense of justice and of love. And in the New Testament, when the Pharisees and Sadducees, presuming upon their chosen status as sons of Abraham, came to John the Baptist for baptism, John said to them: " '. . . God is able from these stones to raise up children to Abraham. Even now the ax is laid to the root of the trees; every tree therefore that does not bear good fruit is cut down and thrown into the fire' " (Matthew 3:9-10). The New Testament affirms that those who bear good fruit do so because they are possessed by the Spirt of Christ, and that the remnant is the Christian community, those who are graced with the gift of membership in the Body of Christ. But Jesus makes clear that such membership is not assured simply because a man says to him, "Lord, Lord," and Silone makes clear that many of Rocco's churchgoing contemporaries go hardly a step beyond the utterance of these words. If sonship to Abraham is not enough for salvation, neither is the presence of one's name on the church roll nor the partaking in the services of the Church.

Christian doctrine distinguishes between the Church Visible, made up of all those belonging to the Church regardless of their degree of loyalty to it, and the Church Invisible, the communion of saints who are the true children of God within the Church. Christian judgment as to the ultimate destiny of a man who would seem to follow in the steps of Christ, but who refuses membership in his Church Visible, is divided. Rocco is such a man, and there is no doubt regarding Silone's view of his destiny: Rocco is a true member of the remnant, destined to live in God's eternal presence; and immortalized with him will be his closest companions in the Italian valley and men and women of their kind from the four imagined corners of the earth. Lazzaro's trumpet, which may not reappear until " 'next year, or twenty or five hundred years from now' " (313), is the symbol of their hope. It is a trumpet with a glorious lineage: the Lord spoke of it to Moses—" '. . . when you go to war in your land against the adversary who oppresses you, then you shall sound an alarm with the trumpets, that you may be remembered before the Lord your God, and you shall be saved from your enemies' " (Numbers 10:9); and Isaiah tells the Israelites that on the day of their deliverance, "a great trumpet will be blown, and those who were lost in the land of Assyria and those who were driven out to the land of Egypt will come and worship the Lord on the holy mountain at Jerusalem" (27:13). Lazzaro's trumpet, it should be remembered, is the one which seemed to one of the novel's characters to resemble the Day of Judgment and the Last Trumpet.

The time to which Silone and his dispossessed characters look is the final Day of the Lord, a day which springs from the inspired imagination of an apocalyptic vision. It will be then that all those who have struggled faithfully and indefatigably in the name of the Lord, all those who have known that the saddles of this imperfect world are no places for prophets, and all those who endure all forms of derision and persecution as a result of their protest against injustice—it will be then that Lazzaro's trumpet will be sounded for the last time, summoning the remnant to the kingdom prepared for them from the foundation of the earth. The words of the prophet Micah, certainly music to the ears of Rocco and his kind, may serve as a fitting conclusion and a concrete picture of that condition which must always remain invisible to earthly eyes:

> It shall come to pass in the latter days
>> that the mountain of the house of the Lord
> shall be established as the highest of the mountains,
>> and shall be raised up above the hills;
> and peoples shall flow to it,
>> and many nations shall come, and say:
> "Come, let us go up to the mountain of the Lord,
>> to the house of the God of Jacob;
> that he may teach us his ways
>> and we may walk in his paths."
> For out of Zion shall go forth the law,
>> and the word of the Lord from Jerusalem.

He shall judge between many peoples,
    and shall decide for strong nations afar off;
and they shall beat their swords into plowshares,
    and their spears into pruning hooks;
nation shall not lift up sword against nation,
    neither shall they learn war any more;
but they shall sit every man under his vine and under his
        fig tree,
and none shall make them afraid;
    for the mouth of the Lord of hosts has spoken.
For all the peoples walk
    each in the name of its god,
but we will walk in the name of the Lord our God
    for ever and ever.
In that day, says the Lord,
    I will assemble the lame
and gather those who have been driven away,
    and those whom I have afflicted;
and the lame I will make the remnant;
    and those who were cast off, a strong nation;
and the Lord will reign over them in Mount Zion
    from this time forth and for evermore.
And you, O tower of the flock,
    hill of the daughter of Zion,
to you shall it come,
    the former dominion shall come,
    the kingdom of the daughter of Jerusalem. (4: 1-8)

HADDAM HOUSE BOOKS